# BOSTAN-E-SAADI

**IN THE NAME OF GOD, THE MERCIFUL,
THE COMPASSIONATE**

# THE ORCHARD:

## THE BOSTAN
## OF SAADI OF SHIRAZ

Translated from the Persian

by

**Mirza Aqil-Hussain, Barlas**

THE OCTAGON PRESS
LONDON

ISBN 0 863040 34 9


**Published with the aid of a subvention
from The Sufi Trust**


Published in 1998


Printed and Bound in Great Britain at
Redwood Books, Trowbridge, Wiltshire.

In the name of **The Sustainer of the world**\* and **Creator of life**
So wise that He has created the power of speech in human tongues.
He is the **Possessor, Bestower** and **Helper**
Who is **Liberal, Pardoner of sins, Acceptor of excuses**
So exalted that whosoever might turn his face from Him
Would have no honour at any door he visited.
Heads of haughty monarchs
Bow humbly to the ground of His mansion in supplication:
He does not catch the arrogant suddenly
Or turn away the contrite with violence:
If He becomes angry at wrongdoing
Whenever you abstain He forgives the past.
If someone became quarrelsome towards his own father
The father would undoubtedly be wroth with him:
If one's own became angry
He would turn him away like an alien.
If an active and alert servant would not work
His master would not keep him in esteem.
If one is not kind to friends
The friends will stay at a distance[1].
If a soldier leaves his post
The king has no responsibility towards him.
But the God of the high and the low
Did not stop anyone's bread on account of his disobedience.
Both the worlds[2] are but a drop in His ocean of knowledge:
He sees the faults and indulges them with clemency
The surface of earth is His general table[3] —
Friends and the foes are alike on it.
If he desired to catch hold of the cruel ones
Who would have escaped the severity of His hand?
His being is free of the calumny of contemporaries and opposites,
His land independent[4] of the obedience of man and jinn.

\*All the emphasised words are Islamic attributes of God.

Everyone and everything obeys His orders,
The progeny of Adam, the birds, the ants and the flies —
He spread out such a vast and broad table of generosity
That the Simurgh[5] of the Caucasus eats its bread from it.
So kind, so generous, fulfiller of tasks
The guardian of His creations and knower of their secrets
He deserves supremacy and to be known
Because his land is old and His Self independent[6].
One He adorns with the crown of fortune
One He destroys and ruins from a throne
One He caps with good fortune.
To someone a rag of misfortune
Makes the fire a garden for Khalil[7]
And sends a group to hell through the Nile's waters[8]
If that[9] was a mandate of His beneficence
This[10] is His command of anger.
He sees evil deeds, even those behind curtains
He forgives with His kindness.
If He drew His sword only to warn
Even the closest and most pious angels[11] would become deaf and dumb;
And if He announced that He was going to be generous
Even Satan would say that He wanted his share.
In His great royal court of kindness
Eminent elders have shown humbleness[12].
Nearer the humble in **His Divine Blessings**
And **Acceptor** of the supplications of the humble.
Potential happenings are in His knowledge
And His penetrating knowledge aware of untold secrets
By virtue of **His Nature** He is the guardian of the earth and the heavens.
He is the **Judge** of the Day of Judgement
There is none who is not obligated to Him
And there is none to find fault with Him.

*All the emphasised words are Islamic attributes of God.

He is **The Eternal, The Well-Wisher** and **The Lover of Virtues.**
By his order the imprint of being takes place in mothers' wombs.
The sun and the moon from the east to the west
He made them travel and spread the earth on water;
When the earth was rendered miserable from fever and trembling
The nail of the mountains was driven into it.
He accords the impression of a fairy to the sperm —
Who has done painting on water (other than God!)
He creates the ruby and the turquoise inside the stone
And a red flower on a green bough,
Throws a drop from the clouds into the sea
And from the spinal cord the sperm in the womb.
A lustrous pearl is created by that drop
And a tall and graceful being by this sperm.
Even the secret of an atom is known to Him
For Him the open and the closed are one and the same.
Provider of food to the snakes and the ants
Howsoever weak and helpless they may be.
By His command non-entity became entity[13] —
Who knows how to make something from nothing other than Him?
Again He will take you to non-existence
And from there to the field of general resurrection.
There is anonymity about His powers
Humility in truth about His intrinsic worth:
The human being cannot comprehend anything of His **Majesty**[14].
Eyesight cannot reach the limits of His elegance;
The bird of imagination cannot reach the pinnacle of His substance[15]
Nor could the hand of understanding reach the skirt of His qualities[16].
Thousands of boats sank in the whirlpool of knowledge of God
Even a single plank from them did not appear on the shore.
Many nights I sat in contemplation
Fear caught hold of my sleeve and asked me to arise.

*All the emphasised words are Islamic attributes of God.

His knowledge encompasses the universe —
Your imagination cannot comprehend it:
Knowledge cannot understand the substance of Truth
Neither can meditation reach His profound attributes.
In eloquence and rhetoric one can reach the status of Sahban[17]
But cannot reach the Truth of the **Incomparable Holy God**.
The virtuous have ridden horses in this path
But in accordance with LA AHSA[18] have remained frustrated in the race —
A horse is not run at every place
But on many occasions one has to throw off the shield[19].
If some devotee[20] discovers the mystery
His way of return is closed;
He is given a goblet[21] in this assembly
In which the medicine of oblivion is mixed.
Some falcons[22] have their eyes sewn
One has his eyes open but feathers burnt:
No one found the way to the treasure of Qarun[23]
Or if he found the way, he did not return.

I died in the waves of this sea of blood
From which no one took his boat —
If you are desirous of crossing this way
Then first cut off the legs of the horse of return,
Reflect in the mirror of your heart
Slowly and steadily attain perspicuity.
Perhaps the fragrance of love will make you intoxicated[24],
Make you a claimant of the covenant of Alast[25].
With the feet of search[26] you will travel thus far
And from this place you will fly with the wings of love;
Your positive knowledge will rend the veil of imagination
No curtain shall remain excepting Majesty.
Then there is no speed for the conveyance of wisdom

*All the emphasised words are Islamic attributes of God.

Astonishment will hold its reins and say, "Stop!"
No one except the guide[27] went into the sea
He was lost who did not follow the Shepherd[28].
Those who have become apostates from the path,
They have travelled too much and have become distracted;
Whosoever went against the way of the Prophet
He will never reach his destination.
O Saadi, do not think that the way of salvation
Can be trodden without following the footsteps of Mustafa[29].

## GLOSSARY

(1)   Lit. *farsang*, A Persian measure of distance. One *farsang* is equal to approximately three miles.

(2)   This world and the world hereafter.

(3)   *Safra* or *Khwan-e-Yaghma* is a cloth spread on the ground for eating food.

(4)   Independent means free. Viz., He does not need the men and the jinn to be obsequious to Him.

(5)   *Simurgh* is a legendary bird in the Caucasus mountains.

(6)   Free: see note 4.

(7)   *Khalil* means a friend. It is the title of Abraham — Ibrahim Khalil-Allah, friend of God. He is said to have been thrown into a fire by order of the Egyptian Pharaoh, but the fire, miraculously, turned into a bed of flowers for him.

(8)   The Egyptian soldiers tracking Moses were drowned in the Nile waters.

(9)   The story of the Prophet Abraham when the fire became a bed of flowers.

(10)  The drowning of the soldiers sent by the Pharaoh in pursuit of Moses. See note 8.

(11)  Lit. *Karr-o-Bayan*: A group of angels not concerned with the policies of the universe.

(12)  Lit. have thrown off their grandeur.

(13)  According to Islamic belief there was nothing — no sun, earth, moon, or stars. There was a void when God commanded *KUN*, (Be), and everything was created.

(14)  Viz. human beings could not comprehend the majestic and the glorious display of God's beneficence.

(15) Human imagination cannot reach the zenith of Nature.

(16) He is beyond comprehension.

(17) Sahban ibn-Wail was a famous orator of Arabia. There is a play on words here: Sahban is the orator and Subhan is a name of God.

(18) There is a tradition of the Holy Prophet saying: "*LA AHSA SANAUN ALAIK*" meaning, "Verily, I find myself incapable of comprehending your praises".

(19) Have to be humble and powerless.

(20) Literally *Salik* : devotee of the path.

(21) Goblet of the knowledge of God.

(22) Hunting falcons' eyes are sewn up in their early training. Here it means a saint who has not achieved the light of the Knowledge of God.

(23) Qarun was an immensely rich man. Here it means the treasure of the Knowledge of God.

(24) Will make you drunk with the love of God.

(25) According to the Traditions of the Prophet, God assembled all the souls on the Day of Genesis and asked: "*ALAST BI RABBIKUM?*" = "Am I not your Lord?", upon which they unanimously replied "*BALAA*" meaning "Verily It Is Thou". This is called the covenant of Alast.

(26) Desire.

(27) Guide here means the Prophet.

(28) Shepherd here means the Prophet.

(29) A name of the Prophet.

# IN PRAISE OF THE HOLY PROPHET
## (CHIEF OF ALL THINGS THAT HAVE BEEN CREATED)
## MAY THE CHOICEST BLESSINGS OF GOD BE ON HIM

Of noble manners and talented virtues
Messenger of all created things, recommended of, recommender of adherents
Patriarch of the messengers and guide of the way
Trusted of God, sanctum for the descent of Gabriel
Advocate of all things that have been created, leader of the day of general
    resurrection
Chief of righteousness and presider over the court of resurrection
Such a speaker with God that the highest heaven is his Tur[1];
All lights are but the shadows of whose resplendence
Such an orphan that without reading the Quran[2]
He set aside[3] the libraries of many a religion.
When his resolution drew the awe-inspiring sword
By a miracle he divided the moon into two pieces[4];
When his fame spread on the face of the earth
There was an earthquake[5] in the palaces of Khusrau[6];
By exclaiming La (no), the height of Lat[7] diminished
By exalting the faith, the honour of Azza[8] was lost:
Not only were Lat and Azza disgraced
But the Torah and the Bible were annulled.
A ride by night took him higher than the heavens;
In grandeur and dignity he surpassed the angels
So fast did he travel in the field of His closeness
That even Gabriel was left behind at Sidrat-ul-Mantaha[9].
The Chief of the Ka'aba said to him:
"Come forward, O messenger of God's revelations
When you found me sincere in friendship

Why have you turned your reins from my company?"
He replied, "I have no strength or ability to go any further —
I became tired as I failed to find any strength in my arms;
If I flew higher by even the breadth of a hair
The Brightness of Manifestation would burn my wings."
No sinner would remain in bondage
Who has such a leader and precursor —
What eulogy of choice should I offer you.
Salutations upon you, O prophet of all created things
May the salutations of God bless your soul
And your companions' and followers' (souls):
First is Abu-Bakr, the elderly companion and disciple
(Then) Omar, twister of the arms of the rebellious monster;
Osman, the wise, awake all night in prayer
The fourth is Ali, the king, rider of Duldul[10].
O God! Through the agency of the progeny of Fatima[11]
On the words of belief[12], bring me to an end:
Whether you accept my prayers or reject them
I will hold the skirt of the descendants of the prophet.
O auspicious presider, what impediments would get in the way
Of your exalted status at the court of Allah The Eternal
If a few faithful beggars
Would gain through your help the hospitality of paradise?
God has praised you and made you respected
He made Gabriel kiss the earth of your status in your honour;
The high heavens are humble in comparison with your dignity.
You were born while Adam was still in his constituent elements of water
    and clay:
You were the first[13] to come into substance and existence

Whatever came into existence later was a branch.
I do not know what praises to shower on you
For you are higher than whatever I would say.
For you the honour of *Lou laak*[14] is sufficient,

# PRAISE

It is sufficient to say *Taha*[15] and *Yasin*[16] in your praise.
What praises should this incompetent Saadi shower upon you
O *Nabi*[17], praises, blessings, compliments and the salute on you.

# GLOSSARY

(1) *Tur* is the mountain where Moses had converse with God.

(2) It is customary for children to read the Quran, but the Prophet was not literate and he was also an orphan.

(3) Literally : washed aside.

(4) A miracle of the Prophet. He asked the moon to split asunder "on the orders of God' and it was seen to part and remain in two pieces for some time.

(5) Fourteen minarets of the palace of Khusrau, the Persian emperor, fell down on the day the Prophet was born.

(6) Title of the Persian emperors.

(7) Name of an idol inside the Ka'aba before the advent of Islam.

(8) Another idol in the Ka'aba.

(9) *Sidrat-ul-Mantaha* = the place in the seventh heaven which even the most pious angels cannot cross. The Holy Prophet, exclusively, passed through it.

(10) Duldul was a mule given to Ali by the Prophet.

(11) Fatima was the daughter of the Prophet. She was the wife of his companion Ali and the mother of Imam Hasan and Imam Hussain. Her progeny are the Sharifs or Sayeds, accorded the highest honours in the Islamic community, above kings and royalty. Royal titles and kings are in any case forbidden by Islamic Law.

(12) It is given in the traditions of the Prophet that whoever says "There is no God but One God" will enter paradise (*Mishkat*).

(13) It is given in the Traditions that God first created the light of the Prophet.

(14) It is given in the Traditions that God said, "I would not have created the earth and the heavens if it had not been for you".

(15) One of the titles of the Prophet. (These are Quranic mystic words appearing in Surah XX and Surah XXXVI).

(16) One of the titles of the Prophet.

(17) O Messenger of God!

# REASONS FOR COMPOSING THE BOOK

I roamed the world extensively
And spent my days with various people,
I benefited from every corner
And I gleaned[1] from every collection;
Of a humbler and holier disposition than the people of Shiraz[2]
I did not see, may God bless that land.
My attachment to the men of this spotless place
Made me dissatisfied me with Sham[3] and Rum[4].
I did not like the idea that from those gardens
I should return home to friends empty-handed.
I thought: people bring sugar from Egypt
And take it as a gift to friends;
But even if my hand were empty of that sugar
The eloquence that I have is sweeter than sugar:
Not such a sugar as people will apparently eat
But one which companions of inner qualities would inscribe on paper.
When I ventured into this palace of wealth
I erected ten doors[5] of instructions:
The first chapter pertains to justice, prudence[6] and counsel
Guarding the created and the fear of God;
The second foundation I laid was of beneficence[7]
Because the grateful thank God for His favour;
The third is about love[8], inebriation with the love of God[9] and zeal[10] —
Not the love which unnecessarily occurs in someone[11];
The fourth about humility[12] and the fifth on contentment[13]
The sixth about the contented ones
The seventh chapter about the state of training[14]
And the eighth on gratefulness for welfare;
The ninth about rectitude and the way of penitence

And the tenth in supplication and on the completion of the book.
On the august day and blessed year
On an auspicious date in between two Eids[15]
Fifty-five was added to the sixth century[16]
When this famous treasure became full of pearls.
Listen, O wise one of happy augury —
I did not hear any skillful person as a caviller[17] —
Whether your shirt is silk cloth or of fine painted Chinese silk[18]
There would of necessity be padding in it.
If you are the one with fine painted Chinese silk on, do not try to vex —
Be kind and keep my padding concealed.
I am not proud of the means of my eminence —
I have extended my hand for charity.
I have heard that on the day of resurrection
God will pardon the sinners along with the virtuous;
If you chance to detect anything wrong with my poetry
By the virtues of the Creator of the World, adopt politeness;
If you like even one verse out of a thousand
By your generosity, refrain from fault-finding[19].
No doubt, my composition in Persia
Is valueless, like musk in Khotan[20].
Like the sound of the beating of a drum, my reputation was only from a
    distance
My imperfection was hidden in a small bag.
Saadi has brought flowers into a garden
And pepper to India with boldness[21].
The skin of the date is full of sweetness
But when you remove it, there is a stone within.

## GLOSSARY

(1)  Literally in Persian: *Khirmane khushae yaftam. Khirmane* means a heap or stock
      of unthrashed corn; *khushae* is an ear of corn; and *yaftam* means 'I found.'

(2)  Shiraz is a famous city in Iran, the home town of Saadi.
(3)  Syria.
(4)  Central Asia, Turkestan.
(5)  The book contains ten chapters.
(6)  In the Persian, *Tadbir*; which here means prudence. *Tadbir* can also stand for management and policy.
(7)  Literally in Persian : *Ihsan* (from Arabic) = beneficence or benevolent actions.
(8)  Arabic: *Ishq* = love. Here it means the love of God.
(9)  In Persian: *Masti*, which means drunken with the love of God.
(10) Persian: *Shur*, which is allegorical for zeal.
(11) Carnal love.
(12) Arabic: *Tawazu* = humbleness and modesty.
(13) Arabic: *Rada* = contentment.
(14) Education or instructions.
(15) *Eid* is a Muslim festival. The first Eid falls immediately after the fast of the month of *Ramadan*. It is celebrated on the first of the succeeding month, *Shawwal*. The second Eid is called *Eid al Adha*, and is celebrated on the tenth of the month of *Zil Hijj*. Between *Shawwal* and *Zil Hijj* falls the month of *Zi-Qaad*.
(16) 655th year of the *Hijrat* or Emigration of the Prophet from Mecca to Medina. The present work, the *Bostan-e-Saadi*, was completed in the month of *Zi-Qaad* in the year 655 *Hijri*, which corresponds with the year 1257 of the Christian Era.
(17) Critic.
(18) Persian: *Purnian*, a fine painted Chinese silk.
(19) Criticism.
(20) Musk was produced in large quantities in the area of Khotan.
(21) Pepper was imported from India into Iran.

13

## NARRATION OF THE VIRTUES
## OF SAAD ZANGI'S SON ATABAK[1] ABU BAKR
## MAY GOD KEEP SAAD'S GRAVE PURIFIED!

My temperament was not inclined towards this mode:
I did not have the intention of eulogizing kings
But if I versified using the name of a certain person[2]
Perhaps pious people would say after me
That Saadi who scored in rhetoric
Lived in the times of Abu Bakr ibn-Saad.
It is appropriate if I be proud of his times
Like the Prophet[3] was of the times of Nausherwan[4].
Ruler of the world, defender of the faith and the just
None like Abu Bakr was born after Omar[5] —
Leader of the exalted and the crown of the elders:
O World, take pride in the times of his justice.
If someone wants protection from sedition
He will find no place of greater security than this country:
It is glad tidings to a door which is like the Holy Ka'aba —
People from far-off places crowd to it[6].
I never saw such treasure, country and throne
Which is an endowment for the children, the mendicant and the aged alike;
No afflicted person came before him
To whose heart he did not apply salve;
He is a seeker of good, and is hopeful —
O God, fulfil all his expectations!
The point of his cap reaches high into the skies
Yet, from modesty, his head is on the ground:
Modesty in the exalted is praiseworthy —
The humility of the mendicant is his habit
What if the humble adopts humility?
But the powerful one who adopts modesty is devout indeed.
Report of his refined manner does not remain a secret

15

And his generosity and graciousness are renowned in the world.
Such wise men of auspicious nature
Cannot be recalled from earlier times.
You will not find a person oppressed in his time
Who is outraged by any aggressor;
Such customs, arrangements and order were not seen by anyone —
Faridun[7] in spite of his pomp and show did not see them.
On account of this, his rank of honour is exalted before God
For due to his dignity the hands of the weak are strong;
He projects his shadow on the world in such a manner
That even an old woman is not afraid of a Rustam[8].
People have always, because of the vicissitudes of fortune,
Lamented over the vagrancy of the times[9]
But, O King, during your reign of justice
No-one has any complaint about the times.
I see the world living comfortably during your era:
I do not know what will happen to the people after you.
It is due to your auspicious times and prosperity
That Saadi is living in your reign:
For so long as the moon and the sun are in the skies
There is eternal mention about you in this book.
If kings gather renown and reputation
They learnt the way and manners from their predecessors.
You, in the conduct of your kingship
Have taken precedence over your predecessors;
Alexander[10] by means of a wall of bronze and stones
Narrowed the way for Gog[11] in this world.
For you, the wall for the Gog of Paganism[12] is gold[13],
Not a bronze wall like Alexander's.
The linguist-poet who, during this reign of justice and peace
Does not thank you — may he lose his tongue.
What a sea of bounty and a mine of beneficence —
Due to your being does the human gain in strength.
The attributes of the king are beyond reckoning:

This petty volume cannot contain them.
If Saadi comes to dictate them all
He will have to open a new archive.
I have become unpretentious in giving thanks for these favours —
It were better if I raised my hands in supplication:
May the times remain according to your desires and the heavens friendly
    to you!
May the Creator of the World guard you!
May the world keep your sublime star bright!
May decadence burn the star of your enemy!
May you be free from the vicissitudes of the times
And no anxiety pollute your heart!
Because a little grief in the hearts of kings
Causes distress in the hearts of all the world
May your heart remain collected and your country inhabited!
May dispersal not afflict your people!
May your body remain upright like faith!
May the heart of your enemy remain as dull as his scheming!
May your inwardness[14] remain delighted by the help of God!
May your heart, faith and land always remain prosperous!
May the Creator of the World pour down upon you His mercy!
Whatever more I say is a fable and fiction —
It is sufficient for you that from glorious God
You have more divine guidance for good.
Saad Zangi did not leave the world afflicted
When he made a renowned Khalaf[15] like you —
Not surprising that this branch is from that very chaste root
Whose soul is in the heavens and whose body is in the earth:
O God, on that famous and renowned grave
Shower the rains of mercy, by Your Grace!
If a likeness and memory of Saad Zangi remains
Then may the heavens assist Abu Bakr's son Saad.

# GLOSSARY

(1)  *Atabak (Atabeg)* (Turkish) = the sovereign, "Father of Lords".

(2)  Abu Bakr Ibn-Saad Zangi. (*Ibn* signifies the son of).

(3)  The Prophet Mohammed lived during the times of Nausherwan "The Just", Emperor of Persia.

(4)  A celebrated Persian king of the Sasanian dynasty. Imam Hussain, grandson of the Prophet, married the daughter of the last Sasanian Emperor.

Hence the Saadat: (Descendants of the Prophet) Sayeds, all now trace their descent both from Hashim the Arab of the Koreshite lineage, and also from the Iranian imperial line.

This is one reason they are accorded royal honours in Islamic communities.

(5)  The Caliph Omar. He was the second caliph of the Rashida Caliphate and a companion of the Prophet.

(6)  An Arabic couplet. The Ka'aba is the square, black-draped cubical building in Mecca, the centre of the Great Mosque.

(7)  Faridun, a celebrated Iranian (Persian) king of the Kianian dynasty. He overcame and ousted the tyrant king Zuhhak from the throne.

(8)  Rustam, the famous warrior and wrestler described in the *Shahnama* (Book of Kings) by Firdausi. Here the sense is that even an old woman was not scared of a dangerous person like Rustam due to the all-prevailing justice of the king.

(9)  Persian. Literally : all the time people from oppression of the times; Lamented and from the vicissitudes of fortune.

(10)  Alexander the Great.

(11)  Gog and Magog are traditionally the progeny of Yafath (*Japhet*), son of the prophet Noah, living in the northern mountainous regions. This tribe used to plunder the people of the plains. Alexander the Great is credited with building a wall of bronze and stone between two hills and thus stopped their access to the plains.

(12)  Gog of paganism = the Mongols.

(13)  The *Atabak* of Shiraz was a feudatory of the Mongols.

(14)  Inwardness = the innermost consciousness, the soul.

(15)  *Khalaf*: a successor.

# IN EULOGY OF THE PRINCE OF ISLAM
## SAAD IBN¹ ABU BAKR IBN-SAAD
## SAADI SAYS :—

Fortunate youth enlightened in mind
Young in monarchy but mature in prudence
Ripe in wisdom and lofty in resolution
Courageous in arm and intelligent at heart:
Fortunate is the mother of times
Who nourishes such a stream[2] in her bosom.
Through liberality he humbled the river[3],
Surpassed the sublimity of the Pleiades with his magnanimity,
How fortunate that the whole kingdom intently looks towards you
The exalted necks of despotic rulers[4].
The oyster that you see full of pearls
Is not as precious as one inimitable pearl —
You are that fine[5] peerless gem
Which is an ornament of the house of monarchy.
O God! Keep him safe before You[6]
Save him from any harm from an evil eye.
O God! Make him universally renowned
Make him respected through obedience to divine guidance;
Make him stable in justice and in piety
Fulfil his desires in this world and in the life hereafter.
May you not have grief from your despicable enemies
May the vicissitudes of the times not inconvenience you.
The tree in paradise bears fruit like you
The renowned son of an illustrious father:
Regard that family as foreign to wellbeing
Which speaks evil of this dynasty.

What faith and wisdom — what justice and redress
What a country and what wealth which by the grace of God, shall
    remain everlasting.

# GLOSSARY

(1) Ibn = son of. Referring to the son of Abu Bakr ibn-Saad Zangi, the subject of the previous chapter.

(2) The king is metaphorically described as a stream.

(3) I.e. in generosity he surpassed even the river.

(4) I.e. how fortunate that the necks of all exalted monarchs are intently looking towards you. I have translated the text reading:—

*Zahe chashme daulat ba ruyi tu baz*
*hama shahr yaran e gardan faraz*

but in some manuscripts this verse is given thus:—

*Zahe chashme daulat ba ruyi tu baz*
*sare shahy-yaran-e gardan faraz*

In this case the translation of the first part of the verse would be:—

So exalted is your dignity that the eyes of the monarchy are fixed on you.

And the second part of the verse would mean:—

The heads of arrogant despots are at your lintel.

(5) Persian — literally : "You are that hidden single pearl."

(6) Persian — literally : "O God! Keep him safe before Your eyes."

CHAPTER ONE

# IN CONNECTION WITH JUSTICE, COUNSEL AND THE MANAGEMENT OF GOVERNMENT

## IN CONNECTION WITH JUSTICE, COUNSEL AND THE MANAGEMENT OF GOVERNMENT

The benign favours of God are beyond conception
What service can this tongue, full of gratitude, render?
O God, keep this dervish-loving king
Under whose shadow is respite for all creatures
Long at the head of the created ones!
Keep his heart immortal with the divine guidance of obedience!
Make him fortunate enough to gain from the tree of expectation!
Make his head green[1] and face white, full of lustre with Your divine mercy!
Do not tread the path of ceremoniousness, O Saadi
If you have sincerity then simply bring it and come (without ceremony).
You recognise the destination and the king is a wayfarer;
You are the veracious one and the king listens to the truthful
What need is there that the nine seats of heaven[2]
Be put under the foot of Qizal Arslan[3]?
Do not say, "Put your foot of grandeur on the heavens[4]":
Say rather, "Put the face of selfless adoration on earth".
With obedience put your face at the door of God —
That is the way for the sincere;
If you are an obedient person keep your head at this door
And throw off the cap of sovereignty from your head[5].
When you worship do not put on royal dress:
Weep and wail like a sincere dervish —
"O God! You are wealthy
You are the powerful supporter of the dervish.
Neither am I the king of the land nor do I command —
I am one of the beggars at this door.
What comes out of my hand and conduct?
Yes, if Your hand of kindness becomes my helper
Afford me an opportunity to act devoutly and with goodness.
What goodness, otherwise, can I render to anyone?"

22

In the night pray with passion like beggars do
If you want to act as a king during the day.
The haughty are alert at your door —
Your head should be on the threshold for prayers.
That king is good for his obedient subjects
Who performs his duty towards Allah.

## GLOSSARY

1) Viz. keep him young and his hair black.
2) When the king knows the facts there is no need to exaggerate like Zahier Faryabi, the poet, who eulogized Qizal Arslan, the king.
3) Qizal Arslan: a renowned king.
4) Viz. do not teach him haughtiness.
5) Viz. there should be humility and modesty in Divine worship and not vanity.

## A LEGEND

I watched a man from the plains of Rudbar[1]
Come riding on a leopard before me —
Seeing which I became so terrified
That fear tied my feet from fleeing[2].
He smiled and put his hand to his lips.

O Saadi! Do not be surprised whatever you may see.
Neither must you turn your face from the commands of God
No one will turn his neck from your orders —
When the king runs according to God's commands
Then God is his Guardian and Helper.
When God keeps you as a friend, it is impossible
That He will leave you to the hands of the enemy.
This is the way: do not turn your face from it —

23

Step forward and get whatever you wish.
He will be benefited by advice
Who likes Saadi's sayings.

## GLOSSARY

(1) Rudbar is a famous riverside town between Gilan and Qazwin in Iran.
(2) I was so surprised that I stood there and gazed.

## KHISRAU'S[1] ADVICE TO HORMUZ[2]

I have heard that in the agonies of his death
Nausherwan[3] spoke thus to Hormuz:
Look after the heart of the dervish
And be not anxious about your own comfort;
No one will have any respite in your country
If you want only your own comfort.
No wise person would like it
If the herdsman[4] were asleep and the wolf was in the midst of the sheep.
Go — have consideration for the needy dervish
For the king is the crowned head of his subjects:
The subjects are like roots and the king like a tree
O son, the tree becomes strong through its roots.
Do not, for so long as you can, injure the heart of the people
If you do, you extirpate your own roots.
If you want a straight way
The way of the virtuous is through expectation and fear[5]:
He should not like to cause injury to people —
Otherwise who will be afraid of loss of repute in his own land
If he has not this in his disposition?
If not, there would be no aroma of contentment in that country.

24

If you have responsibility, give a thought to their contentment,
If you are unattended, keep to your way.
Do not look for prosperity in that country and territory
Where you find its subjects displeased with their monarch.
Beware of presumptuous and arrogant people —
Be afraid of those who are not afraid of God:
Then you will see that country peopled in your dreams only
Which keeps the hearts of the inhabitants miserable.
Oppression brings misery and infamy —
The righteous have reached this conclusion after much thought:
The people should not be subjected to oppression
For they are the sheet-anchor and the support of the government.
For your own sake take care of the peasants
Because a happy-hearted labourer does more work:
It is against courtesy to do evil to someone
From whom at times you have received benevolence.

## GLOSSARY

1) Khisrau was a title of the Persian kings; here, however, it means Nausherwan.
2) Hormuz was the son of Nausherwan.
3) Nausherwan: a celebrated Persian king of the Sasanian dynasty.
4) I.e. the king becomes careless and tyrants start oppression.
5) It is a saying of the Prophet that it is for a true Muslim to remain fearful of chastisement from God and hopeful of divine mercy.

## KHISRAU'S ADVICE TO SHEROYA[1]

I have heard that Khisrau told Sheroya
At the time when his eyes started sleeping from seeing[2]:
Be true to whatever is your moral code
Keeping in mind the welfare of your subjects

25

Do not turn your neck, O son, away from wisdom and advice
Lest people walk away from you[3].
People run from a tyrant:
Making his ugly name known all over the world
So that soon he extirpates his own roots.
Whosoever has laid an evil foundation
The lion and the swordsmen bring (it) destruction
But not as much as the smoke[4] from the hearts of the children and the
    women.
The lamp kindled by a widow —
You may have seen that it burnt down an entire town.
Who is more fortunate in the world than one
Who, in governing his territory, lived with justice?
When the time came to depart from this world
People showered divine blessings on his grave.
Since both the good and the evil have to die
It is better that people mention your name with benevolence.
Set a Godfearing person over the citizens
For a pious person is the architect of a country.
He is malevolent to you and cruel to the people
Who seeks pleasure in tormenting creation —
It is folly to entrust authority to such a one
Due to whose deeds people's hands are raised in invoking God[5].
A protector of the good never has to face evil
If you protect the evil you are an enemy of your own life.
Do not requite your enemy only with money —
His very root should be extirpated from its very foundation:
Do not be lenient with cruel administrators
The skin must be flayed from the corpulency (of such a one).
The head of the wolf must be severed before
Not after he has savaged the goats of the people.

## GLOSSARY

(1)  Sheroya was the son of Khisrau Parvez, grandson of Hormuz and the great-grandson of Nausherwan. *Oya* means like. *Sher-oya* therefore, means 'like a lion'.
(2)  Closing on account of approaching death.
(3)  From your deeds.
(4)  Metaphor for the signs of distressed hearts.
(5)  Due to his evil deeds, people would raise their hands in misery to beseech God to rid them of the tyrant.


## A TALE

Well did a captured trader speak
When thieves surrounded him with arrows aimed:
'When thieves start performing acts of bravery
Then the men of the army and the body of women are akin."
The king who harasses merchants
Closes the door of well-being on the city and the army;
No sensible person will then venture there
When they hear reports of the bad conditions.
If you want renown and approval for goodness
Negotiate with merchants and porters fairly:
Respectable people hold travellers in high regard
Because they spread their renown all over the world;
That kingdom will be ruined very quickly
From whence travellers return in distress.
Acquaint yourself with the poor and be a friend to the pilgrim
Because the pilgrim is the one who spreads fame:
Look after guests better, and hold dear the traveller
And be heedful of any hardships suffered by them.
It is better to keep aloof from strangers
Because one may be an enemy in the guise of a friend.

Raise the dignity of your old people[1] —
There will never be a betrayal by one who was fostered
When any of your attendants becomes old:
Do not forget to pay his yearly rights[2].
If old age has tied the hands he used to attend on you
You still have the power of generosity.


## GLOSSARY

(1)   Literally : your ancients.
(2)   Yearly rights are pensions given to old attendants.


## A TALE

I have heard that Shahpour[1] remained silent
When Khisrau[2] struck off his name[3].
When destitution made him wretched
He wrote this epistle to the king:
"O King! Dispensing justice to the horizons of the world —
Though I did not remain (in office) you remain (on your throne) in your
    excellence:
As I spent the season of my youth in your service
Do not remove me from before you in my old age.
That foreigner whose mind is full of mischief:
Do not harass him but turn him out of the country —
It would be proper if you were not angry with him
Because his own bad habit is ever his enemy.
If his native land is Persia
Do not send him to Sanaa[4] or Saqlab[5] or Rum[6],
Do not even let him seek shelter during the warm morning:
It is not proper to set loose a fiend (misery) upon others

For they would curse saying, 'May calamity overtake that land
From whence such people come!'
If you want to assign work, search for an unselfish person:
Because the indigent one has no fear of the king,
When the indigent one commits some error
Nothing shall come out of him other than groaning and wailing.
When the chief officer of the state relinquishes his trusteeship
A supervisor should be appointed there:
If he also starts intrigues for his own benefit
Remove the work from both the chief officer and the supervisor.
The trustee to be appointed should be God-fearing —
Do not appoint a trustee who is afraid of you only:
Investigate and count[7] and sit thoughtfully
Because you will not find one (good) trustee in a hundred.
Two mature people from the same tribe, trade and profession
Should not be sent to a place to work together:
How would you know if they became accomplices and friends?
One may turn thief while the other shields him.
Fear and discontent amongst the thieves
Makes possible a safe escape for the caravan.
The one you have deposed from high rank
When some time passes, pardon him.
To solve the problem of a supplicant
Is better than to release a thousand prisoners.
Make a good accountant the centre of the work —
Neither will he err nor cut the rope of expectation.
With compliant people, the administrator of justice, the king
Should get angry like a father with his son —
Sometimes he beats him so that he starts crying,
Sometimes wipes his eyes clear of tears.
Continuous mildness makes an enemy bold
And if you remain angry they will become tired of you:
Sternness and mildness mixed together are good
Like a surgeon who operates and then dresses the wound.

Be bold, of pleasant manners, liberal and generous;
What God bestows on you, offer to your subjects in turn.
When you remember the reigns of earlier kings
Let there be read similar writings after your own reign.
Nobody came into the world and lives forever
Excepting he who leaves a good name behind —
He did not die who left these behind as his heritage:
Bridges, tanks, alms-houses and rest-houses.
He who left behind no successor
His tree of existence bore no fruit.
If someone dies and does not leave selflessness and happiness
No prayers[8] should be offered after his death.
If you want renown in the world
Do not obliterate the good name of your ancestors —
They also had their desires, whims and cheerfulness:
At last they left, leaving everything behind;
One took back a good repute from the world
One left behind a bad custom for ever.
Do not listen to anyone's backbiting with pleasure
If it is told to you then try to penetrate to its origin;
Accept a guilty person's plea of forgetfulness —
If he seeks to be pardoned, excuse him.
If some guilty one seeks shelter
It is not proper to kill him for the first fault
But (only) when he has been warned and paid no heed:
The alternative for him is prison in fetters.
If even advice and fetters prove to be of no avail
It is a wretched tree: extirpate it!
When you become angry with someone's failing
Reflect deeply before inflicting punishment:
For it is easy to break a ruby from Badakhshan[9]
But a broken one cannot be made whole again."

## GLOSSARY

(1)   Shahpour was Khisrau's vizier (Prime Minister) who arranged his meeting with his beloved Shirin.
(2)   Khisrau was a title of the Persian kings.
(3)   Dismissed him.
(4)   Sanaa, the capital of Yemen.
(5)   Saqlab is a town in Asia Minor.
(6)   Rum is Byzantium, now Turkey.
(7)   The cash in the treasury should be checked often.
(8)   Literally : *Alhamd* — a name of the verse in the Quran meaning "Praise be to Allah, Lord of the Worlds". This is recited in every prayer and also when someone dies.
(9)   Badakhshan is a province of Afghanistan bordering China, famous for its ruby mines.


## A STORY CONCERNING ADMINISTRATION BY KINGS AND DELAY IN POLICY MATTERS

A man came from the river Umman[1]
He had travelled extensively through deserts and rivers
And had seen the Arabs, the Turks, the Tajiks and Rum[2].
He had knowledge of all kinds in his pious mind
Having journeyed the world accumulating wisdom,
Widely travelled and brought up in good society
In appearance he was strong, like a stout tree.
But due to extreme circumstances he was destitute:
Two hundred patches one sewn on top of the other
Scorched in the middle from the heat.
From the riverside he came to the city —
There was a powerful king in that territory
Who was renowned for his good disposition
With humble entreaty he would place his head on the feet of dervishes.
The king's attendants washed him —

31

His head and body from the dust of the way.
(To pay his respects) he put his head on the threshold of the king's court
And speaking benedictions he put his hand on his chest[3]
Saying: "I did not find, in this empire anywhere
I went, anyone distressed with an afflicted heart;
I found nobody drunk or intoxicated
But I did find the taverns ruined:
For the king this arrangement of affairs is sufficient
That he should not be pleased by anyone's suffering."
He spoke as if showering pearls from the skirt of his robe
With such eloquence that the king was greatly impressed.
He admired his power of speech
Called him near and honoured him
Welcomed him, thanked him for his visit, gave him gold and pearls
Enquired of him his lineage and his native land.
He replied to whatever was asked about his adventures
And attained more closeness than others with the king.
The king thought in his heart:
"Such a person is worthy of the premiership of the country
But gradually, so that the people of the court
Do not oppose my judgment.
First, I must test his intellect
Then I must increase his status according to his virtues.
Grief oppresses his heart
Who does any work without experimenting:
When a Kadi[4] writes a document with close attention
He does not suffer shame and disgrace before the learned.
Reflect while the arrow is within your thumb
Not at the time when you have released it.
Like Youssef[5], one has to be virtuous and discerning
Has to spend many years before becoming an Aziz[6]
Over a long period of time."
It is not possible to plumb the depth of anyone's character:
He investigated everything about his morals and ethics —

He was a sagacious and mannerly person of religious disposition.
The king found him to be of pious nature with enlightened mind
A wise and prudent person, knowing the dignity of man;
In judgement he excelled the elders.
The king made him sit above his vizier[7], higher in rank:
He showed so much wisdom and skill
That his decrees[8] did not break the heart of anyone;
He brought the country under his control
And he did not earn the displeasure of anyone.
He closed the mouths of all the critics
For not a single bad word for anyone came from his pen.
The envious found he had not embezzled even a single barleycorn
Rolling about like an ear of wheat was not useful for him
Through his genius the government attained splendour.
A new grief came to the old vizier[7] —
He did not find any defect in the wise new one
With which he could reproach him:
The faithful and the malicious are like a large basin and an ant
Which cannot bore a hole through it by force.
The king had two slaves, with faces bright like the sun
Who always remained by his side, on the alert[8]
Both of them pure and chaste like a houri[9] or fairy
Like the sun and the moon, unparalleled,
With faces such that you would say one was not better than the other —
In the mirror they showed themselves alike.
The sweet talk of the intelligent one
Affected the graceful cypress-like[10] figures of both:
Discovering that the morals and ethics of this man were good
Spontaneously they became his well-wishers and friends.
Philanthropy and benevolence affected him too
But not that tendency which affects the indiscreet with depravity —
He felt only solicitude when
He saw their faces.
If you want your position to be exalted

Do not become attracted, O master, by young beardless ones;
If some of your own desire does not intervene
Avoid it because it is detrimental to your dignity.
The vizier[7] got some hint of this
Out of wickedness he took it to the king:
"I do not know what people call him and who he is
He does not want to live with honour in this country.
I have heard that he is inclined towards your slaves —
He is a treacherous and a lascivious person.
Foreigners live a heedless life
Because they were not brought up in this country and this court.
Such an immodest and impudent person is not proper
He will bring bad repute upon the king's palace.
I would definitely be neglecting the favours of the king
If I kept quiet when seeing depravity.
These are not rumours hurriedly related
I did not speak to you until I was certain —
One of my servants has heard
That he was in amorous indulgence with one of these two.
I have stated facts and now I leave it to the king's judgement —
As I have tested, do you also put it to the test."
With wickedness and mischief he explained in full detail —
May a fortunate moment never come to the evildoer
When the evil-minded get the upper hand in affairs
Inflaming the heart of the elders with fire.
A tiny spark can light a fire —
The old tree can be burned then.
At this the King swelled with rage
As angry as if a reaping sickle had hit his head.
In his rage he wanted to spill the blood of the dervish[11]
But patience restrained him from doing so.
It is not manliness to kill someone you have fostered
It is a mistake to be cruel after being kindly.
Do not harm the one you encouraged

When he is holding your quiver do not strike him with an arrow;
He should not be raised up in favour
When you want to suck his blood cruelly.
Until you were certain of his virtues
He did not become your favourite in the royal palace:
Until you are certain of his guilt
Do not harm him because of the complaints of detractors.
The king kept this secret hidden in his heart
Because he had listened to the words of the wise.
O wise man! The heart is the prison for a secret —
Once revealed, you cannot draw it back (even) with chains.
He observed the work of the dervish surreptitiously
And found flaws in the conclusions of the intelligent one.
Suddenly he glanced towards one of the slaves —
That fairy-faced one smiled with lips closed.
Two persons who have an understanding
Can talk between themselves and yet remain silent.
Do you know that a person observing unobtrusively
Becomes not sated, like a dropsical one full from the river Tigris?
The king's suspicion of vice became a certainty —
Rage made him desire to become furious
But even then, he restrained himself with sound policy and perfect judgement
Said to him slowly, "O person of good repute!
I took you to be a wise man with sense
Made you a trustee of the secrets of the government;
I thought that you were wise and imagined you prudent
I did not take you to be immodest and detestable.
Such an exalted position is not your place —
It is my miscalculation and not your fault;
Definitely when I patronise a lowborn one, then
He would be likely to be treacherous to my women's apartments."
The intelligent one raised his head
And said to the learned king,
"When the skirt of my garment is free of crime

35

I do not mind about the wickedness of the evil-minded
But I had never presumed this evil opinion of me.
I do not know who said such a thing[12] which was far from my mind."
The angry king said that the vizier[7] had told him:
"Do not make an excuse now and find a pretext."
The dervish smiled and put his hand to his lips:
"Whatever he says should not astonish me!
The envious person, seeing me in his place —
What other than evil and backbiting can come from his tongue?
I had considered him an enemy from that moment
When the king made him sit below me;
When the king gives me precedence over him
Doesn't the king understand that he is an enemy of mine?
He cannot take me as a friend till the Last Day
For he sees my glory as an insult to him —
About this I want to tell you a story
If in the beginning you would listen to this servant."

# GLOSSARY

(1)    The Gulf. Also the name of a town near the sea-coast.
(2)    Asia Minor.
(3)    It is customary in the East to place one's hands on the breast as a mark of respect while speaking with elders.
(4)    *Kadi* = judge.
(5)    Joseph, the son of Isaac, who later became king of Egypt.
(6)    A title of the ancient Egyptian kings.
(7)    Prime Minister or Premier.
(8)    Literally : *Amr-o-nahiesh* = to enjoin right and forbid wrong.
(9)    *Houri* = a creature of the light in paradise.
(10)  Since it is a tall, evergreen tree, it is considered graceful in the East.
(11)  The man who had come from the Gulf.
(12)  That is to say that I am not in love with either of the two slaves nor was I holding either of them in my embrace.

36

## A PROVERB

A man saw Satan himself in a dream
In stature he was tall like a pine tree and his face was (shining) like the sun;
Seeing him he exclaimed, "O one resembling the moon
People knowing naught of your comeliness
Thought that you had a dreadful face,
Made hideous pictures of you in the Hammams[1]."
Satan laughed and said that it was not his own work
The pen had been in the hands of an enemy.
'I had them ejected from paradise[2]
Now from animosity they think me hideous."

'Similarly, I also have a good name:
My adversary does not say so out of malice
The vizier[3] whose reputation has been ruined through my increase in
     dignity —
One must run a league away from him and his artifice.
But I am not afraid of the king's wrath:
A person without fault is intrepid in his speech —
When truth flows from my pen
Why should I flinch from criticism?
The worker who has not blundered in his dealings
Is not afraid of the accusation of his fellows.
If the superintendent of weights and measures comes in for an inspection
     he should be anxious
Whose measures are faulty."
The king was amazed and perplexed upon hearing this
He began to repent; rubbing his hands despite the dignity of his sovereignty.
So that the culprit, should not by artifice and impudence
Go free for the crime committed by him, he said:
"I have not only heard it from your adversary[4] —
Have I not seen you with my own eyes?
Out of those assembled in this court

37

Your eyes fall on no one other than these two."
The eloquent person laughed and said:
"There is a point in it if you would graciously listen —
May your wisdom increase and the State remain firm!
Have you not seen the helpless dervish sometimes
Observing the rich man with envy?
The strength of my adolescence has left me —
The days of youth were lost in skipping and jumping.
I cannot restrain myself from looking at them
Because they are the bearers of beauty and elegance;
I too had a bright and delicate flowerlike face
In comeliness my stature was also like crystal glass.
Now at this extremity I must become a shroud[5]
For my hair is (white) like cotton and my body thin as a weaving spindle.
I too had curly hair black like the night,
The tunic lay tight to my body, elegant;
I had teeth on both sides of my mouth
Standing like a wall of silver bricks:
Now look at me as I speak —
Each fell like an old bridge.
Why should I not look at them with longing and regret
As I remember my ruined life;
Those dear days left me
Suddenly this day will also end."
When the wise man had braided these pearls of intended sense
The king said that it was impossible to speak any better[6]
He looked towards his courtiers:
"Do not look for better words and (meanings)
Such a one is entitled to look towards a beloved object
Who knows how to vindicate himself so successfully.
If by reason of my understanding I had not been mild to him
I would have persecuted him on the word of his adversary.
Swift drawing of the sword in rage
Takes one's repenting back of the hand towards the teeth[7];

Do not listen to the talk of the one who has an interest
Because if you were to comply you would repent."
The well spoken-of person received dignity, respect and wealth —
The evil-spoken one was punished.
Due to the counsel of the sagacious vizier
The king's name gained renown in the country;
With justice and graciousness he ruled for many years.
He died and left behind a good reputation.

Such kings who are the protectors of the faith
By the power of faith take the authority of state.
In these days I do not see any of them
If there is one — it is Abu Bakr Saad only:
Intelligent sovereign, fortunate and prosperous!
May the bough of his expectation yield fruit.
O King! You are (as) the tree of paradise[8]
Casting your shadow on a course one year long (like the sun).
I had the ambition that my fortunate star
Would cast the feather of Huma[9] on my head
But intelligence says that the Huma does not bestow wealth —
If you want prosperity, come under this shadow.
O God! Yours has been the Divine Mercy
That You have cast this shadow on the people;
Like a slave I am a wellwisher of the state
O God! Keep this shadow lasting and steady
It is better to imprison before sentencing to execution
Because the severed head cannot be replaced.
One having authority, judgement and nobility
Is not dejected by the outcry of the people.
A head full of vanity and devoid of tolerance:
It is forbidden to put a crown on that head.
I do not say that you adhere to war[10]
But when anger wakens keep your senses in their proper place —
One with understanding has patience

39

Not an intellect which is subdued by anger:
When anger runs its forces from the valley
Neither justice nor piety or faith remain —
I have not seen a demon of like nature under the skies
Which makes so many angels run away[11].

## GLOSSARY

(1)   *Hammams* = Turkish baths. It was customary in those days to draw frightening pictures of Satan on the walls of the Hammams, to warn against immoral thoughts or acts.
(2)   According to Muslim mythology, Satan deceived Adam into eating the forbidden food whereupon Adam was turned out of paradise.
(3)   The old vizier.
(4)   "I did not believe the word of the old vizier but I have seen your actions with my own eyes."
(5)   The greying of the hair and the thinning of the body in old age signify that death is approaching.
(6)   The new vizier had answered the king so beautifully that he was completely satisfied.
(7)   In the East the act of repentence is signalled by biting the back of the hand with the teeth.
(8)   *Tuba* = a tree in paradise. Its shadow is so long that it takes a year's journey to traverse it.
(9)   The *Huma* or Phoenix is a legendary bird. It is said that whoever comes under the shadow of its feathers becomes a king.
(10)  It is not as difficult to make a stand in battle as it is to control anger.
(11)  When the human being is saturated with anger the angels of Divine Mercy flee away.

## DISCOURSE

Is it not true that without permission from the Divine code of law[1] the
    drinking of water is forbidden
And if you kill another according to a judicial decree it is legal[2].

40

If the Divine court decrees death
Do not hesitate to kill the man.
If you discover others in his family
Forgive them and give them respite:
The transgressor was blameworthy —
Why should the poor women and children pay a penalty.
Your body is strong and you have powerful forces
But do not take them into the opponent's territory
Because he will take refuge in a high fortress
And a guiltless country will suffer the consequence.
Investigate the condition of captives —
In all probability some innocent ones may exist there.
If a foreign merchant dies in your country
Misappropriation of his goods would be an ignoble act
For when people cry over him
Then your own kinsmen and his family would say together
That the poor fellow died in a foreign country
And a cruel person took away whatever effects he had.
Reflect on the fatherless child
And avoid the burden of repercussions from the sighs of his wounded heart.
Sometimes good deeds carried out over fifty years —
One evil deed ruins all that reputation.
The eternally renowned, the chosen
Did not seize the money of the common people;
Though he be a king to the horizons of the world
When he snatches the property of the rich he is a beggar:
The fearless one (may) die of wretchedness
But he did not take advantage of the poor.

## GLOSSARY

(1)    Literally : *Shar'a* = the Divine code of law.
(2)    Literally : *Fatwa* = a judicial decree in accordance with the Divine Code of
       Law. It is forbidden to drink water during the month of Ramadan while fasting.
       If, in accordance with the Divine Code of Law, one slays someone, the slayer
       will be rewarded.

## A STORY

I have heard that a just king
Had a long gown with lining on both sides
Someone said, "O good-natured, great king!
Have a gown sewn of Chinese silk brocade."
He replied, "This much is good for covering and for comfort —
Anything further is ornamentation and decoration:
I do not raise revenues
To beautify myself, the throne and the crown.
If, like ladies, I adorned a suit of clothes
How could I then repel the enemy with manly vigour?
I have hundreds of yearnings and desires
But the treasury does not belong to me alone;
Revenues are collected for the army
And not for decoration and ornamentation:
A soldier who is not happy with the king
Cannot guard the frontiers of his country —
When an enemy robs the villager of his ass
Why does the king collect the revenue and the tithes?
When an adversary takes away the ass and the king (the) revenue
What prosperity can one see for that throne and crown?
It is inhuman to show force to the powerless —
The mean bird snatches the grain from the ant.
Subjects are like a tree if you patronise them —
You will eat its fruit as if invited by friends
But do not dig at its roots and fruit cruelly
Because the fool repents later, alone.
Fortunate, they eat fruit from their youth
Who do not use force and violence on their subordinates.
If some dependant stumbles
Be afraid of his weeping and crying before God;
If you can conquer a country with softness
Do not shed any blood by fighting even from a single pore

To the manly, kingship of the whole earth
Is not proper if even a drop of blood falls to the ground."


## A STORY

I have heard that the auspicious Jamshed[1]
Had this engraved on a stone near a spring:
"Many like me took rest at this spring
And left in the twinkling of an eye;
We took the world by valour and with effort
But could not take it to our graves."

When you gain advantage or power over an enemy
Do not harass him, for this grief itself is too much for him.
A distressed but living enemy around you
Is better than his blood on your head.


## GLOSSARY

(1)   Jamshed was a famous legendary king who reigned for hundreds of years and
      was ultimately killed by Zuhak.


## A STORY

I have heard that Darius of that auspicious dynasty[1]
Became separated from his army during a hunting trip.
A grazier came running towards him —
The emperor took an arrow out of his quiver:
Care is needed against enemies in the wilderness

It is in the house that a flower is free of thorns.
The terrified herdsman clamoured:
"I am not your enemy, do not try to kill me!
I am the one who looks after the king's horses
I attend on them in this pasture."
The king's alarm receded
And he laughed saying, "O, stupid one!
Some heavenly, auspicious angel favoured you
Otherwise I would have pulled the bow-string up to my ear."
The herdsman from the grazing-ground smiled and said:
"A precept should not be concealed from friends —
It is not a sensible policy or credible judgement
For the king not to know a friend from a foe;
To lead the life of a ruler it is a condition
That you know each retainer, who and what he is.
You have frequently seen me at court
Have enquired about the condition of the horses and the meadows;
Yet now that I came before you with kindly intent
You could not distinguish me from an enemy.
O renowned king! I can do this much —
That I can pick one horse out of a hundred thousand horses;
I work as herdsman with understanding and judgement:
You also should hold your flock steadily."

There is danger of disorder and damage in a country
Where the policy of the king is inferior to the shepherd's.


## GLOSSARY

(1)    Darius was the Persian king defeated by Alexander the Great.

## DISCOURSE

How can you hear the complaints from the seekers of justice
When the curtains of your sleeping apartment are near Saturn[1]?
Rest in such a way that the cry of distress can reach you
When some seeker of justice cries out in pain for help
And groans at the hands of a cruel oppressor in your day:
But the cruel one, the oppressor — that is your tyranny.
The dog did not tear the skirt of the caravan —
It was the ignorant husbandman in charge of that dog.

O Saadi, you are presumptuous in your speech:
When the sword is in your hand, then conquer[2].
Tell what you know because it is better to speak the truth —
You are neither extorting a bribe nor swindling;
Keep silence and wash the book with sagacity:
Then leave aside your covetousness and say whatever you wish to say.


## GLOSSARY

(1)   Saturn is supposed to be in the seventh heaven, i.e. very far away.
(2)   Speak on — whatever advice you want to give.


## A STORY

In Iraq a king came to know
That a needy one outside the palace was saying:
"You also are an expectant one waiting at a door,
Therefore fulfil the desires of those lying at the doors —
Liberate the afflicted hearts from their grievances
So that your heart never becomes aggrieved.

45

The perturbation caused by the hearts of the seekers of justice
Pulls down kings from their thrones.
You, sleeping in the cool comfort of your womens' apartment at midday,
Are telling the stranger to get burnt in the heat outside."

God redresses the grievance of the person
Who has not been able to secure redress from the king.


## A STORY

One of the very great
Tells this story of Ibn-e-Abdel Aziz[1]:
He had a gem on his finger-ring
On which the jewellers were unable to put a price:
You would say that, at night, all matter was equally lustrous
Yet that pearl was like daylight in splendour.
As fate would have it there came a year of drought —
The faces of the people became like a crescent instead of the full moon.
When he found neither energy nor relief amongst them
He did not find it compassionate to rest himself.
When someone sees poison in the mouth of the people
How can good drinking water pass his own lips?
He ordered that the ring should be sold for silver
Because he took pity on the strangers and the orphans:
In a week's time the money was dissipated —
He gave it to the dervishes, the poor and the needy.
His critics taunted him,
"You will not get another like that one."
It is related that he replied with tears raining
Down his face like drops on a candle:
"Ornamentation is inhuman for the king
When any citizen's heart is wounded —

46

For me a finger-ring without a gem is acceptable
But not the sorrowing heart of mankind."
That person is better who sees to the comfort of men and women
Giving preference to their comfort over his own;
The wise did not show any inclination
To put their own pleasures before the grief of others.
If the king on his throne sleeps comfortably
I do not think the beggar can sleep content;
If he stays wakeful till late in the night
His people will sleep in comfort and with relief.
Thank God this is the usual habit and straight path
Atabak Abu Bakr ibn-Saad is on —
Nobody sees any signs of sedition and mischief in Fars[2]
Other than the stature of beauties with faces like the moon.
I liked the five verses
Which people were reciting last night at a gathering.


## GLOSSARY

(1)  Refers to Hazrat Omar, son of Abdel Aziz, the second famous caliph of the
     Ummiya dynasty. He is one of the first four caliphs and a Companion of the
     Prophet.
(2)  Fars = Persia.


## DICTUM

Last night I enjoyed the comforts of life
Because one with a face beautiful as the moon was in my arms,
Drowsy and intoxicated with sleep.
I said, "O one before whom even the cypress is low and humble —
Wash the slumber from your narcissus-like eyes for a little while:
Laugh like a flowery bough, sing like the nightingale;

O Seduction[1] of the world, why do you sleep?
Come and bring the ruby-coloured wine of yesternight."
The beautiful one stirred from sleep, saw and said:
"You call me sedition and then say 'Don't sleep!'"
In the times of this enlightened king[2]
Nobody wants to see a different sedition waken.


## GLOSSARY

(1)   *Fitna* means sedition. In Persian there is a play on words: *fitna* is used for a
      'beautiful beloved' since the beautiful one excites the passions and seduces them.
(2)   During the times of Atabak Abu Bakr ibn-Saad Zangi.


## A STORY

It is written in the chronicles of the ancient kings
That when Takla sat on the throne of Zangi[1]
No one was troubled by oppression in his reign —
He would have excelled if this had been his only quality.
Once he said to a pious man,
"My life has been wasted to no effect:
The throne, the grandeur and the country are all things that will come to
      an end —
Who takes any wealth from the world other than a mendicant?
I want to sit in a secluded corner in Divine worship
So that I get something from the remaining days of my life."
When the sagacious and enlightened one heard this
He became severely agitated and said, "O Takla, enough!
There is no (path) other than through the service of mankind;
It is not in the rosary, prayer-mat or a mendicant's habit made of patches,
      shreds and rags

Remain on your throne as the king
And with your chaste virtues remain a dervish.
Keep ready your sincerity and goodwill
Guard your tongue from frivolous talk and pretence;
The way requires action and not pretentiousness
Because reality does not have standing without action.
The elders who had perspicacity
Also had patched and ragged garments concealed under their long gowns."

## GLOSSARY

(1)  Zangi was the second king of Persia of the Atabak dynasty. He died in 510
     A.D. and his son Takla succeeded him.

## A STORY

I have heard that one of the sultans of Rum[1] began lamenting
Before a learned, pious person:
"I do not have any power left because of an enemy;
With the exception of this fort and the city nothing remains to me.
I tried to ensure that my son
Should be the leader of the assembly after me.
Now, that the low-born enemy has gained power,
He is denigrating my valour and manliness!
What should I do; what remedy should I seek?
Grief has wasted away my soul and body."
The wise man frowned and said, "What is this wailing?
One must weep over such intellect and courage.
Why do you rue the sovereignty, grieving
That the better and the greater part of life has come to an end?
While you are alive, there is sufficient for you;

49

When you leave, the world is another person's —
Whether he be intelligent or a fool
Do not fret about him — he will take care of himself!
Sovereignty is not worth enduring hardship[2]
To claim it by the aid of the sword only to leave it.
Make your own arrangements, because that wise man
Who will succeed you will take care of himself.
Be not proud of your five days' stay[3] —
Consider and reflect on your own departure.
Which of the kings of Ajam[4] do you know
Who oppressed their dependants
And where decay did not befall their throne and country —
No sovereignty remains other than the Sovereignty of the Most High God.
Nobody expects to live for eternity
Because this world itself is not eternal.
Whoever owned silver, gold, wealth and riches
After him, it is spent in a few days.
And the one whose goodness continues,
Whose soul receives blessings incessantly —
It is the great man whose good name endures:
It could be said to the pious that he himself remains!
Be aware: if you nourish the tree of liberality
You will indeed eat the fruit of success.
Be generous for tomorrow when comes the reckoning,
The rank of honour will be in relation to the magnitude of their good deeds;
Those who are raised up
Their dignity will be the greater in the royal court of the Most High God.
The ones lagging behind will be faithless and ashamed —
That idle person will seek cover
Leave him so that he bites the back of his hand with his teeth:
The oven remained so hot yet he did not bake bread in it.
At the time of harvest
(He will realise) how negligent it was not to sow seeds."

## GLOSSARY

(1) Rum = Asia Minor.
(2) What one conquers with great hardship and the aid of the sword and then leaves at the time of one's death is not a thing worth taking much trouble about.
(3) Meaning a little time.
(4) Ajam = the non-Arab world.

## A STORY

A man in the wilds of Sham[1] whose name was God's Friend
Retreated to a secluded spot and started living in a cave;
Due to his patience and resignation in that dark corner
He put his foot into the treasury of contentment.
Men of eminence came to his door
Because he would not stoop to anyone's else's door.
The sincere person possessing knowledge of God and His Kingdom, wishes
To give up the inclination to beg and seek charity
When his soul demands every moment of his time:
With disgrace his heart makes him travel from village to village.
Where this holy man lived
There was a cruel governor of the frontier;
Whomsoever he found powerless
He would overpower by force.
He ruined the territory without mercy and was a wicked killer;
Due to his contemptuous nature everyone was made miserable.
Groups of people left the place to avoid disgrace and cruelty
And they spread news of his bad repute in other territories.
Some miserable people, injured at heart, remained
Who cursed him and detested him secretly.
Wherever the hand of cruelty is extended
You will not find peoples' lips open for laughter.
Sometimes he would come to visit the holy man

51

But that friend of God did not pay him any attention.
The ruler once said "O one of good disposition!
Do not turn your face from me with hatred;
I realise that I value your friendship —
Why then should you harbour enmity towards me?
I admit that I am not the chief of the whole territory
But in dignity and honour I am not less than a dervish!
I do not say that I should be treated better than others —
But behave towards me in the same manner in which you treat others."
The pious and learned one heard
And became annoyed saying, "O king, have discernment!
Your being is a misery to all creation
And I do not like the distress of fellow human beings.
When you are an enemy of my friends
I cannot regard you as my friend.
Even if we became friends
God regards you as an enemy!
Even if people were to tear open the skin of God's Friend
He cannot be the friend of his friend's enemy.

I am surprised at the slumber of the hard-hearted
Due to whom the town sleeps in misery
Beware! If you possess skill, wisdom and discernment
Make the effort to be benevolent and compassionate.

## GLOSSARY

(1)   Sham = Syria.

## DISCOURSE

O elder, do not show off your strength on the weak
Because time and age do not remain in a constant relationship.
Do not twist the arm of a weak person
Because if he finds an opportunity he will overpower you at once.
I tell you, do not cause vexation and affront
Because if you stumble you will have no remedy —
It is better to satisfy friends than to accumulate wealth
It is better if the treasury stays empty than that people are troubled.
Do not be indolent in doing another's work;
Maybe you will have to fall at his feet one day.
O weak one! Be careful of the strong
Because some day you will be stronger than he.
Frustrate the contentious with resolution
Because the arm of resolution is stronger than the hand of power.
Do not laugh at the dry and parched lips of the oppressed —
Because they will (eventually) pull out the teeth of the oppressor.
The master woke up at the sound of the kettle-drum:
What did he know of how the watchman passed the night?
The caravan is concerned about its own load —
Nobody sympathises with the wounded back of the donkey.
Admittedly, you are not amongst the fallen ones:
But, when you see the fallen, why are you still standing?
On this I will tell you a tale
Because it would be idleness to leave out the story.


## A STORY

There was such a famine in Damascus
That friends forgot *Ishq*[1].
The skies became so miserly towards the earth
That the vegetation and date trees did not moisten their lips[2];

The old springs dried up
And there was no water except in the eyes of orphans;
There was no flute other than the sighing of widows[3]
If ever any smoke came out of any aperture[4].
I saw trees devoid of leaves, destitute like dervishes —
I saw strong, armed men listless and helpless.
Neither was there green on the mountains nor on the boughs in the gardens
The locusts consumed the gardens and the people ate the locusts.
In such conditions a friend came to me
Whose bones were covered only with skin.
I felt surprised, because his was a huge and mighty frame,
And he was master of dignity, gold and riches.
I said to him, "O friend of pure disposition,
Tell me what ails you?"
He frowned at me and said, "Where is your intellect?
When you know and then enquire, your questioning is wrong!
Don't you see that the calamity has become extreme?
The trouble has reached its climax —
Neither does it rain from the skies
Nor do the sighs of the afflicted ascend to heaven."
I told him, "But you do not have anything to fear —
The poison kills where there is no antidote.
If on account of indigence others have died
You have not, and what fears does a goose have from the storm?"
The sage looked at me sorrowfully
Like a learned person seeing an ignorant one:
"O friend, even if you are on the bank (of a river)
That is no comfort when friends are drowned.
I am not white-faced through destitution —
The needy peoples' affliction has broken my heart.
I do not want any wise person to see a wound
Either on the bodies of others or on his own person.
Thank God, although I am protected against wounds,
When I see (others') wounds, my body trembles;

The composure of a healthy person is disturbed
When he is by the side of a cheerless patient.
When I see that the indigent dervish has not eaten
The morsel in my mouth becomes poison and I grieve.
When you take friends to the prison
What luxury and comfort can remain in the orchard?

## GLOSSARY

1) *Ishq* = love. Sufis used to greet each other saying *Ishq*. Here it means that friends started to avoid greeting each other lest someone asked for something.
2) No rain fell.
3) There were no musical notes.
4) 'Smoke' as an analogy of sighs, from 'burning hearts'.

## A STORY

One evening the fiery[1] and dejected sighs of the populace started a fire
It was said that half of Bagh-e-dad[2] burned.
One thanked God in the midst of the dust and smoke
That his shop did not suffer any damage.
A wise man said to him, "O avaricious fellow!
Your only concern is for yourself
You would not mind if the whole town gets charred
Provided your caravanserai is outside the burnt area!
Who other than a hard-hearted man can fill his stomach
When he sees others with stones[3] tied on their bellies?
How does the wealthy one eat his mouthful
When he sees the dervish eating his own blood[4]?
Do not say that the one who looks after the sick is healthy —
He also writhes in anger and anxiety like the patient.
When the tender-hearted reach their destination
They cannot sleep for thinking of the ones left on the way;
It remains a burden on the heart of the king
That he saw the ass of the woodcutter stuck in a bog.

If there is anybody in the house of good fortune
For him, only a single word from Saadi's sayings is sufficient.
For you it is enough if you listen (to my words) —
If you sow thorns you will not reap jasmine.

## GLOSSARY

(1)   In Persian literature, the sigh is considered 'fiery.'
(2)   The name (Baghdad) was originally Bagh-e-Dad which means Garden of
      Justice. According to legend Nausherwan, the celebrated Persian king, used
      to hold public court here once each week — hence the name: Bagh-e-Dad
      In reality, Baghdad was built much later by the Arabs.
(3)   In hunger, the tieing of flat stones onto the stomach brings relief.
(4)   Eating his own blood = starving and in grief.

## DISCOURSE

Do you know about the kings of Ajam[1]
Who oppressed their subjects?
Their grandeur and sovereignty did not survive
And neither did the oppression of the peasants continue.
Look at the offence which was committed by the tyrants!
The world remained but he rolled together his tyrannies.
The body of the administrator of justice will remain cool on the Day of
      Resurrection
For he will be under the shadow of the throne of God.
For the nation for which God chooses prosperity
To it, He gives a just king of virtuous disposition;
When He wants to destroy some country
He places the territory in the grasp of a tyrant.
People of good disposition contrive deliverance from adversity
Seeing the oppressor as a chastisement from God.

Expect exaltation from Him and be thankful
Because the blessings of heaven vanish with ungratefulness:
Have you not read in the glorious book[2]
That gratitude brings forth affluence?
If you give thanks for this country and its riches
You will obtain riches and wealth everlasting
But if you became unjust in the kingship
You would live on charity after royalty:
It is forbidden for the king to sleep soundly
When the weak are encumbered by the powerful.
Do not cause the people to grieve by even as much as a mustard seed
For the king is the shepherd and the people are his flock:
When they see hostility and injustice from him
Then he is not a shepherd — he is a wolf and they cry out for help.
One, coming to a bad end, his thoughts evil —
He started the custom of oppressing his dependants;
If you do not want people to give you bad names
Be benevolent so that no one can call you bad.

## GLOSSARY

1)   Non-Arab countries.
2)   The Holy Quran.

## A STORY

I have heard that in the region of Bactria
There were two sons from the same father —
Valiant, haughty and gigantic
Handsome, wise and swordsmen.
The father found both of them awe-inspiring

Found them fond of horses and combat.
He divided his country into two parts before his death
Giving a part to each son
In case they fought each other —
In battle drew the sword of malice[1].
After that the father counted the few days (of his life)
And surrendered his sweet life to the Creator of Life.
Destiny, however, loosened the ropes of his expectations
And demise tied his hands of action.
The two kings became established in that kingdom
Because the treasury and the army were boundless.
According to their judgement and for their own advantage
Each adopted his own way:
One dealt out justice, to attain a good reputation
The other oppression, to accumulate wealth.
One made favour and kindness his habit
Spent money and looked after the poor
Erected buildings, gave food to the people for their sustenance and patronised
    the army,
Built rest-houses for indigent dervishes to sleep in at night,
Emptied the treasury and collected an army
Like people do during times of pleasure and enjoyment:
The voices of mirth and joy ascended to the heavens like thunder[2]
As in Shiraz in the times of Abu Bakr Saad,
That intelligent king of good disposition
May God fructify his bough of expectation.
Listen to the tale of that celebrated youth
Who was lucky and auspicious —
He was attentive and showed kindness to the populace,
Praising God in the morning and in the evening.
Wealthy people travelled in security in that country
Because the king was just and the dervish was satisfied.
Nobody was abused during his reign
Not by a thorn and not even by a flower petal.

With acclaim from the country he rose above the elders —
The worthy submitted to his orders.
The other youth wanted to expand his throne and crown:
He increased taxes for the peasants
He became covetous towards the merchandise of the traders
He brought destruction to the wretched poor.
 do not say that he was ill-intentioned towards the dervish —
In fact he was his own enemy:
In the expectation of more and more, he neither favoured anybody nor ate
    himself.
The intelligent people knew that he did not rule wisely;
He accumulated wealth by force.
Having exhausted their patience, the army deserted;
The merchants came to know
That there was injustice in the country of that unskillful king
And they stopped commercial transactions with his country.
Farming did not prosper, the people became discontented
When good fortune became estranged from them.
The foe took the opportunity —
Strife with the heavens extirpated the king
Hooves of the enemy's horses trampled his country
He sought allegiance from those with whom he had broken the covenant
From whom could he expect revenues when all the peasants had fled?
What gain can an evil-minded one expect
Who has maledictions called after him?
When his fortune was topsy-turvy in the word KUN's KAF[3]
He did not do what the virtuous asked him to do.
What did the pious say for that good man:
"You reap the benefit which that tyrant could not exploit;
His vision was wrong and his policy was weak
Because whatever was (to be found) through justice he sought by oppression.

## GLOSSARY

(1)  In order to avoid conflict between the two brothers, he partitioned the country
(2)  The manner in which people shouted and rejoiced during the times of Abu
     Bakr Saad with their shouts ascending to the heavens.
(3)  KUN means 'Be!'. It is in the Holy Quran that whenever God wants to create
     something He commands the word 'KUN' and that thing is created. KUN
     means beginning/eternity and KAF means the first day of eternity/origin.

## A STORY

One sat on a branch and was hacking the trunk;
The proprietor of the orchard saw it and, watching him,
Said: "If this man is doing something wicked, it is
Not against me but against himself."
If you listen to advice it will be your salvation
Do not knock down the weak one with your strong arm
Because tomorrow[1] he will take the king before God —
That mendicant who is not worth a grain of barley in your eyes.
If you want to become a chief tomorrow
Do not make any inferior your enemy:
When your rule is over
That beggar will catch hold of your skirt out of rancour.
Do not put your hand on the poor: withdraw
Because if they felled you, you would have to suffer the humiliation
And it is unbecoming in the eyes of free people
To be disgraced by wretched ones.
The great, enlightened and fortunate
Who by intellect carried away the crown and the throne
Did not stalk honest people with crooked intent[2].
If you want the truth, listen to Saadi.

## GLOSSARY

1)   I.e. on Judgement-day.
2)   Literally : go crooked at the heels of.

# THE ATTRIBUTES OF THE TRANQUIL STATUS OF THE
# CONTENTED DERVISH

Do not say that there is nothing greater than the dignity or the office
of a king
Because there is nothing more happy, auspicious and satisfying than the
     domain of the dervish[1].
The unencumbered go with nimble feet[2]:
That is correct and the pious heed the truth.
The indigent is anxious about a single piece of bread —
The king is anxious about the whole country:
When the beggar gets his evening meal
He sleeps as tranquilly as the king of Sham[3].
Grief and pleasure are both transitory —
With death both these things go out of the head.
What boots it to be crowned by the people?
What merit does he gain, who has to pay taxes?
If there is somebody exalted on the planet Saturn
If there is some destitute one in prison:
When death overwhelms them
You will not be able to tell one from the other[4].

## GLOSSARY

1)   The manifest kingdom is transitory, superficial and likely to decline. But the
     felicity which the dervish acquires through resignation and contentment does
     not decay.
2)   In the Holy Traditions it is stated that the unencumbered attain salvation and
     those with encumbrances are destroyed.
3)   Sham = Syria.
4)   Viz. after death the rich and the poor are alike.

## A STORY

I have heard that once by (the side of) a lake
A skull spoke thus to a pious man:
"I also had the majesty of a crown,
Had a crown of glory on my head:
(Fortune) helped and victory harmonised with me
With the force of my rule I occupied Iraq;
I became greedy and wanted to seize Kirman
When all of a sudden, maggots ate my head[1]."

Remove the cotton of heedlessness from the ear of discretion
So that the advice of the dead may reach your ears.

### GLOSSARY

(1)   I wanted to overrun Kirman but death came to me and maggots ate my head.

## ADVICE ABOUT BENEFICENCE AND EVIL-DOING
## AND THEIR CONSEQUENCES

Nothing malign[1] stands in the way of the pious —
It does not happen that someone practising evil is blessed.
The initiator of a commotion gets involved in the stir
Like a scorpion which seldom returns to its nest[2].
If it is not in your nature to do good to anyone
Then such a pearl and hard stone are nearly the same.
No, O friend of good disposition, I spoke wrongly
Because some profit is derived from iron, stone and bronze.
It is better to die than to be a dishonourable person
Over whom even a stone has preference.
Not every human being is better than a ravening beast
Because a wild animal is better than a bad human being —
An intelligent man is better than a brutal beast
Or a man who ravages human beings.

62

When a man knows nothing other than eating and sleeping
What advantage does he have over animals?
That unprincipled upside-down unlucky rider —
A man on foot outstrips him in a race.
There is no one who sowed the seed of goodness
Who from it did not get a harvest according to his heart's desire.
have not heard ever in my life
Of any evildoer who was rewarded with beneficence.

## GLOSSARY

1) Literally: badness, fault or malignancy.
2) The scorpion bites people and is killed. It seldom has a chance to return to its burrow.

## A STORY

A deceitful and sly ruffian fell down a hole;
In terror of him the lion would become a lioness[1].
The evil-minded one, accustomed only to evil-doing
Had no-one more helpless than himself when he fell
And shouted and cried for help the whole night long.
Not able to sleep, a man hit him on the head with a stone and said,
"Did you ever come to someone else's help
That today you are expectant of help?
Having cultivated the seed of good conduct[2]
Did you then note what a positive response you received!
Who is going to apply balm to your body
When their hearts are still bleeding from the wounds inflicted by you?
You dug the hole in the way for us
And surely you fell into it instead."
Two kinds of people dig a well for the general public:
One of good disposition and the other of ignominious habits —

The first for people to refresh their parched throats
And the other so that people may fall into it headlong.

If you do evil deeds do not expect goodness
Because the seaweed will not bear grapes.
O, one who has cultivated oats during the autumn —
I do not think that you will harvest wheat!
If you nourish the cactus tree with your life
Do not believe that you will ever eat quince seeds from it.
Never will the oleander bough bear dates —
Expect (to harvest) whatever you have sown.

## GLOSSARY

(1)   He was so terrifying a tough that, in his terror even a ferocious lion would become like a meek lioness.
(2)   Said in an ironical way to tease him because he was a man of bad conduct.

## A STORY

It is said that once a pious person
Did not treat Hajjaj Youssef[1] with due attention and ceremony.
(Hajjaj Youssef) looked sharply towards the soldier of the royal court
To spread the leather and to pour sand on it[2].
When an oppressor has no arguments
He makes his face wrathful with disagreement.
The pious man laughed and then cried;
The evil-minded, hard-hearted king was astonished
When he saw first laughter and then the tears
And asked, "What is this laughing and crying?"
He replied, "I weep at the injustice of the times

Because I have four helpless children:
I laugh that by the kindness of holy God
I die as one oppressed and not as an oppressor."
Someone said, "O celebrated king, desist and take your hand from this old
      villager
Because some people depend upon him;
It is not good to kill in haste,
Nobility, forgiveness and benignity should be practised —
Have regard to his young children." The pious one said:
"Perhaps you are an enemy of your own family
That you choose evil for other families;
When hearts are stained by wounds you inflicted, don't think
That on the day of death you will encounter goodness.
The injured one who has not slept: be afraid of his heart-rending sigh
Be afraid of the smoke from his heart in the morning.
Are you not afraid that during the night, a pious one
Might bring forth 'O God!' from a burning heart."
In frenzy he continued to pour out arguments
So that no pretext was left to Hajjaj:
"Does it not happen that Satan did evil and did not see good?
No pure fruit comes from an impure seed:
Do not betray secrets when quarrelling with him
Because some of your faults will be hidden.
Do not challenge brave people with harshness
When you could not win against youths at boxing."
I have heard that the king did not listen and shed the man's blood:
Who can escape the commands of God?
That elderly king did not sleep that night in his anxiety —
He saw the dervish in his dream, saying,
"He could not punish me for long;
Chastisement has been set over him until the day of resurrection."

## GLOSSARY

(1)   Hajjaj Ben Youssef Saqafi was a famous and cruel governor.
(2)   If anybody was executed in open court it was customary to lay down a leather skin and sprinkle sand over it to absorb the blood.

## A STORY

A man was advising his son:
"Remember well the advice of the sagacious —
Do not be violent towards your youngers, O son!
Because some day some elder will clash with you.
Are you not afraid, O stupid son of tender years,
That one day some panther might tear you to pieces?
I was proud of my strength during my childhood
And weaker peoples' hearts were displeased with me:
I received a blow from the fist of the powerful
And I never again tried strength on the powerless."

## DISCOURSE

Watch and be careful that you do not slumber because inattention
Is forbidden to the eyes of the leader of the nation.
Beware, have concern for your subordinates —
Be afraid of the hardness of these times.
The advice which is free of personal considerations
Like bitter medicine repels disease.

## A STORY IN THIS CONTEXT

There is a story about a king
Whom the disease of threads had made thin, like a weaving spindle[1].
His physical debility made him so dejected
That he started to envy even people of low status.
Although the king in chess is renowned on the chess board
When it becomes weak it is weaker than a pawn.
A courtier kissed the earth before the king
And invoking divine favour upon him said, "May the lord live till eternity:
In this city there is an auspicious man drunk with the love of God —
There are few abstemious people like him.
No sooner have people taken their problems before him
Than in a moment they secure their desire.
Call him, so that he cures the disease
And divine blessings may descend from the heavens to earth."
The king so ordered and the chief of the attendants
Summoned the eminent sage.
The king said, "O prudent one, pray for me!
Like a needle, I am tied with this disease of strings."
The old man with stooping back heard this
And in a severe voice, he thundered,
"God is kind towards an administrator of justice:
Be compassionate and then see God's reward!
How could my supplications be useful for you
While the oppressed are in the well and in prisons[2]?
You have not been generous towards creation:
How can you seek tranquillity through intercession?
You must apologise for your mistakes —
Then ask a pious holy man to invoke blessings.
How can his prayers help you
When the curses of the oppressed are still pursuing you?"
When the Ajami king heard these words
He felt sad with shame and disgrace

67

He felt aggrieved but then said, in his heart:
"Why should I be offended, when what the dervish says is right?"
He ordered the release of those in prison.
On his orders they immediately released everyone.
The seasoned sage after two *Rakaats* of prayer[3],
Raised his hands humbly and in an imploring manner towards God,
"O Bestower of exaltation to the skies!
You made him a captive in war, now release him on reconciliation."
The saint's hands were thus raised in prayer
When the patient lying in bed got to his feet
Saying with delight, that he would fly
Like a peacock, for he did not feel 'strings in his legs'.
The king ordered the sacrifice of his treasury of pearls
And people showered offerings over the sage's head and feet.
For the sake of falsity the truth should not be concealed —
He jerked his hem from all that treasure
Saying, "Do not go towards the source of threads again —
Maybe they will raise up their heads again!
When you have fallen once, tread warily
So that you do not once again lose your footing."

Listen to Saadi: Verily
Nobody gets up again after a fall.

## GLOSSARY

(1)     The disease of threads is called Bilharzia in modern medicine.
(2)     In ancient times, hardened criminals were kept confined in wells.
(3)     *Rakaat* = that part of prayer which includes standing, bending and prostration

## DISCOURSE

The world, O son, is not an eternal realm:
There is no expectation of eternity in the world —
Did it not fly in the morning and in the evening,
The throne of Solomon, God's blessings on him?
In the end did you not see that it was thrown to the winds[1]?
He is well-off[2] who passed away full of knowledge and justice;
He won the wager of the state
Who remained anxious for the comfort of mankind.
That came into use which they accomplished[3]
Not that which they amassed and then forsook.

## GLOSSARY

1)  Literally : destroyed.
2)  Literally : cool.
3)  Literally : rolled together.

## A STORY

There was once a great chief in Egypt —
Death marched an army against his life.
Elegance left his warm and cheerful face
Because when the sun grows pale nothing remains of the day.
The intelligent wrung their hands in grief
Because they could find no remedy for death in the science of medicine.
All countries and thrones are transitory and liable to decay
With the exception of the Eternal Ruler's country.
When the day of his life neared nightfall
He could be heard muttering,

"There was no Aziz[1] like me in Egypt
Yet this is the result: there was nothing.
I amassed the world but did not eat its fruit
And I leave it: powerless and frustrated."
He was better advised who was beneficent and ate,
Collected the world for himself[2].
Make efforts while it is yet with you[3]
Because whatever remains undone, there will be regrets and dread[4].
The master in agony of death on his bed
Withdraws one hand and extends the other[5] —
He is showing you with gestures of the hands at that time,
Because dread has stopped his tongue from speaking,
That you extend one hand in benefaction and liberality
And pull back the other from oppression and avidity.
Now while you have it (help someone) —
How will you extend your hand out from your shroud?
The moon, stars and sun will shine for quite some time
But you will not raise your head from your tombstone.

## GLOSSARY

(1)  Aziz is said to have been a title of the ancient Egyptian kings.
(2)  I.e. by doing good deeds collected the treasure for the life hereafter.
(3)  I.e. while you are alive, the world is with you.
(4)  Because at the time of death you will repent over your life and will be in fear
     of accountability before God.
(5)  Usually in the agonies of death a man withdraws one arm and extends the
     other. From it the metaphor is that by extending one arm he means benefaction
     and by withdrawing the other he means withdrawal from oppression and greed.

## A STORY

Qizal Arslan[1] had a strong fort
Which held its neck higher than the Alwand[2] mountains —
It did not fear attack from any quarter and was self-sufficient.

The way leading to the fort was a coil within a coil like the lustrous curly
    locks of a bride —
It looked so wonderful in a setting abounding in verdure
Like an egg on a green plate.
I have heard that an auspicious and well-bred person
Came to the king from afar,
Having knowledge of God and experience
Accomplished and widely travelled;
He laughed and said, "This fort is delightful
But I do not think that it is safe[3] too.
Did your predecessors not win it?
They stayed for some time and then forsook it;
Will your successors not own it after you
And eat the fruit of your tree of expectation?
Remember the reign and the country of your father
But liberate your heart from the bondage of anxiety.
Circumstances made him sit in a corner in such a way
That he did not possess a single copper coin.
When he finally despaired of everything and everybody
He laid his expectations on God's kindness only.
For a sensible person the world is like straw —
In every time there is a place for others."

## GLOSSARY

(1)    Qizal Arslan was a famous Seljuk king of Persia.
(2)    Alwand is a famous mountain in Persia. Here the meaning is that the fort was
       so high that even the peaks of Alwand were lower.
(3)    It will not be able to save you from the assault of death.

## DISCOURSE

Thus spoke a daring person in Ajam[1]
To Khisrau[2], "O successor to the country of Jamshed[3],

If world and fortune had co-operated with Jamshed
How could you have obtained succession to the crown and the throne
If you happened to possess the wealth of Qaroon[4]?
That also will not remain but for whatever may be your benefactions.


## GLOSSARY

(1)  Ajam = non-Arab country.
(2)  Khisrau was a title of the Persian kings.
(3)  Jamshed was a celebrated king of Persia.
(4)  Qaroon was a very rich person who would never give any alms.


## A STORY

When Alp Arslan[1] surrendered his life to the Creator of Life
His son and successor put the crown on his head.
After retiring from the throne and the crown, Alp Arslan was laid to rest
    in a grave
Where there was room neither to sit nor to walk.
An intelligent person, distraught, said
When he saw the son riding horse the next day,
"What an inverted world and times these are:
The father has left and the son's foot is in the stirrup."
Such are the vicissitudes of fortune,
Swift, treacherous and unstable —
When the aged come to the end of their time
An energetic youth raises his head from the cradle.
Do not be attracted to the world because it is an alien:
It moves like a musician from one house to the next.
It is not expedient to enjoy life with such a ravisher of hearts
Who has a different husband every morning.

Be virtuous this year while the village is in your possession
Because next year somebody else will be its owner.


## GLOSSARY

1)   Alp Arslan was the father of Qizal Arslan.



## A STORY

There was a despot in the area district of Ghaur[1]
Who would catch the donkeys of the villagers for forced labour
To carry heavy loads without fodder or grass:
The poor animals died in a day or two.
When circumstances make some ignoble person rich and powerful
He becomes a burden upon the dejected hearts of the fakir;
When the terrace of some conceited person is on a higher level
He throws urine and rubbish onto the adjoining lower storey.
I have heard that once
The cruel king went out to hunt.
He followed a quarry without rest;
Night fell and he had left his train of servants far behind.
All alone, he could recognise no one nor find the way.
Despondently, he stopped at a village at sundown;
He saw an ass which was swift and efficient
Robust, strong and capable of transporting loads.
A Kurd with a bone in his hand
Was beating it so severely as to break its bones.
The king was enraged and said, "O young man,
Your violence has gone beyond the limit on this dumb and helpless animal:
If you have strength, do not be proud of it,
Do not show it off on these poor creatures."

The Kurd did not appreciate this worthless talk
And shouted at the king wrathfully:
"I have not done this willingly or without reason.
When you do not know about a thing, mind your own business!
Very many people whose acts may not seem justified to you —
If you will observe them closely you will find that their action was
    expedient[2]."
The king felt his harsh words
He said, "What justification do you see? Tell me
Because I think that you are alien to reasoning:
Not only devoid of sense, but also mad."
The Kurd laughed and said, "O ignorant Turk, be silent!
Perhaps you have not heard the story of Khizr[3];
Nobody calls him a madman or devoid of sense —
Why did he break the boat of the destitute one?"
The king said, "O cruel one,
What do you understand why Khizr did that?
There was a cruel person in those seas:
Due to him hearts were troubled
The inhabitants of the isles lamented because of him;
A world was upset by him, like a stormy sea.
He broke the boat as he found it expedient
So that the tyrant chief did not seize it.
The broken property that is in your possession
Is better than having it reach the hands of the enemy in a sound condition."
The enlightened villager laughed
And said, "Then the truth is with me, O King
I am not breaking the leg of the ass through ignorance
But due to dread of a tyrant king.
Here a donkey, invalid and lame
Is better than as a burden carrier to the king.
Why do you not tell him who seized the boat
How much disrepute will be his until the Last Day?
I spit on a country and government such as he runs;

The disgrace will remain on him till the Day of Resurrection.
The tyrant is cruel to himself[4]
Not to his poor subordinates
Because tomorrow in that congregation of honour and disgrace[5]
He will hold the collar and the beard with his hand.
Weeping, he will load the burden of his sins onto his own neck[6]
And will not lift his head because of his disgraceful deeds.
I know that now the donkey transports his burden
How will he transport the burden of the donkey on that day[7]?
If you ask — honestly, he is an unfortunate person
Because for his comfort others suffer inconvenience.
These few days are the days of his pleasure
Because his pleasure is in bringing grief to others.
If that hopeless fellow does not awaken from his sleep
Because of him, the people will sleep disheartened."
The king heard all this and did not reply;
He tethered his horse and put his head on the felt cloth of the saddle to sleep
But the whole night long he was awake, counting stars:
In confusion and anxiety he could not sleep.
When he heard the morning bird song
He forgot the perplexity he had experienced in the night.
His horsemen searched for him the whole night long
In the morning they recognised the tracks of his horse.
They saw the king and the horse in a field
And all the soldiers came running.
In respect they bowed their heads to the ground —
The earth became like a river with the waves of men.
The men of rank sat and called for a tablecloth to be spread on the ground
      for serving food;
They ate and drank and convened a meeting.
As the king reflected upon the tumult and merriment of the festivities
He remembered the villager of the previous night:
He gave orders and the soldiers searched and found and held him firmly,
Threw him at the foot of the throne in disgrace.

The executioner pulled out a sharp sword —
The poor fellow found no way of escape;
He comprehended that it was the last moment of his life
And whatever came to his heart he blurted out.
Have you not seen that when the knife is put to the head of the reed pen
The point of the pen runs swifter?
When he saw that he could not escape
He used all the arrows from his quiver fearlessly[8]:
He raised his head despairingly and said:
"It is not possible to sleep in the village in the night assigned for a sleep
    in the grave
Owing to the cruelty that marks your reign.
The reputation of your cruelty is known throughout the world.
I am not the only person injured at your hands
But all of creation; take then one dead from all the creation!
It is surprising that my words hit you so hard —
If you can, kill then all the creation
If my exposition has displeased you
Then try to be just and extirpate the root of evil-speaking:
You should contrive to disarm oppression
And not to kill a poor, innocent man.
When you have been an oppressor, do not then expect
That your name will bruited abroad with goodness.
I do not know how your eyes sleep
When persons aggrieved by you do not sleep.
Understand! Or do you think the king is admired?
When the people praise him in Court —
Of what use is the admiration of a congregation
When men and women reprove him behind his back?"
The tyrant despot listened
From the stupor of pride he suddenly came to his senses.
In the village where his fortune had shown betterment
He awarded the chieftainship to the villager.

You may learn wisdom and the code of morality from the learned
But not as much as from an illiterate fault-finder.
Hear about your conduct from your enemy because in the eyes of your friends
Whatever is done by you is acceptable to them.
Admirers are not your friends —
Your detractors are your friends:
The ill-tempered gives a better reprimand
Than the cheerful sweet-natured friend.
No one will give you better advice than this:
If you are intelligent, one hint is sufficient.

## GLOSSARY

(1)    Ghaur is in Afghanistan.
(2)    Though you will find their action apparently wrong, when you observe them closely you realise that it was prudent.
(3)    Syedna Khizr is the prophet who guides people.
(4)    Since tyranny will stand indicted on the Day of Judgement, he was cruel to himself.
(5)    Doomsday.
(6)    The burdens of the oppressed will be laid on the neck of the oppressor.
(7)    The Last Day.
(8)    He became desperate.

## A STORY

When the reign of the caliphate came to Mamun[1]
He purchased a slave girl with a face as beautiful as the moon
And compared to her face, she was as the sun and in regard to her
      body like a blossoming branch;
Playing with the wisdom of the intelligent,
Her hands dipped in the blood of suitors[2]

77

Her finger-tips of red,
Her eyes azure, her eyebrows captivating the pious
Appearing like a rainbow on the sun.
Came the night, that doll from the progeny of houris
Did not give herself to the embrace of Mamun.
A huge fire of anger flared in his heart:
He wanted to cleave her head in two pieces, like Gemini.
She said, "Here is my head, cut it with a sharp sword
But please do not try to sleep or sit with me."
He asked, "Who has tortured your heart;
Which of my habits has been offensive to you?"
She said, "Even if you kill me and tear open my head —
I am offended by your bad breath."
The arrow shot in war and the sword of oppression kill in an instant
But bad breath is persistent.
The well-disposed king hearing this
Became perplexed and very distressed.
Although at the time his heart felt affronted
He applied medicine and perfume and became like a rosebud[3].
The fairy-faced one became his associate and friend:
"As she pointed out my fault she is my friend."

In my opinion he is your wellwisher
Who would warn that such-and-such a thorn stood in your way;
Taking a wrong path and being told that one is right
Is great tyranny and a great injustice.
When your faults are not pointed out to you
Through ignorance you could regard them as your skills.
Do not say that honey is sweet and that sugar surpasses all
To the person whose need is for scammony.[4]
How truly spoke a chemist one day:
"If you want a cure, take bitter medicines
Strained in the sieve of knowledge
And mixed with the honey of divine worship."

## GLOSSARY

(1) Mamun was the son and successor of the famous Caliph Haroun el-Rashid.
(2) She had applied henna to her hands — hence the metaphor.
(3) By applying medicine and perfume, his bad breath was dealt with.
(4) A bitter purgative.

## A STORY

I have heard that with a pious person, a fakir
A great king became displeased —
Perhaps some just statement came from his lips.
The king was offended through arrogance
And sent him to prison from the court,
Because the arms of the king are strong.
One of the fakir's friends said to him secretly,
"Talking like that was not expedient." He answered:
"To tell the truth is divine worship —
I am not afraid of prison because it is but for a little while."
News of this secret talk
At once reached the king's ears.
He laughed and said, "He has fanciful ideas —
He does not know that he will die in prison."
A page took this message to the dervish
Who said, "O page, tell the king
That the world itself is transitory —
Grief and delight are as nothing to a dervish;
I am not made happy if you patronise me
And I am not troubled if you behead me.
You have the army, the power and the riches
And I have a family, misfortune and wretchedness —
Once we enter the gate of death
We will be equal within a week[1].

79

Do not put your faith in this transitory wealth
Do not burn your body with fire
Your predecessors amassed no more than you
But they oppressed and pillaged the world;
Spend your life in such a way that people remember you with goodness
So that when you die they shall not curse your grave.
Bad traditions should not be made into laws
So that people execrate you and curse the person who made them.
If a strong person vanquishes all
Does not the earth of the grave eventually subdue him?"
That tyrant, by way of oppression, ordered
That the fakir's tongue be torn from his throat.
The man knowing his fate said,
"Whatever you have ordered, I am not afraid.
I am not worried about becoming tongue-less
Because I know that *He* knows, even without my speaking:
If I have to suffer indigence and outrage
Of what concern is that if there is a good outcome.
A time of lamentation is also a festivity
If you attain a favourable end."

## GLOSSARY

(1)   Within a week the bodies will decompose.

## A STORY

A boxer did not have the means to make a living
Neither had he the necessary preparations for his evening meal nor
    arrangements for his breakfast.
He used to carry soil on his back due to the tyranny of his stomach[1]

Because it is difficult to earn a livelihood through boxing[2].
Always, due to the vicissitudes of fortune
His heart was distressed and his body afflicted:
Sometimes he would rail against the treacherous times,
Sometimes he had a sour countenance through ill fortune;
Sometimes on seeing the sweet luxuries of others
Spittle would drip down his mouth as if it were sour.
Sometimes he would bemoan his fruitless endeavours:
"Nobody saw anyone leading a tougher life —
People eat honey, chicken and roasted lamb
Yet my greens do not see the face of bread.
If you look for justice, it is not fair
That I am naked and the cat has fur garments.
Alas, had heaven guided me
So that some wealth had come into my hands
It would have satisfied the longings of my heart for a time;
It would have knocked some of the dust from my toils."
I heard that as he dug the earth one day
He discovered a rotten skull
Its garland broken in the dust[3].
The pearls of teeth had fallen
The tongueless mouth seemed to speak advice and secrets:
"O man! Appease your disappointment —
Is this not the condition of the mouth buried in the dust.
Take it as having eaten sugar or the hearts blood.
Do not lament over the vicissitudes of the times
Because sometimes it is unreasonable to do so."
Then and there as this came into his mind
Worries ceased to encumber his heart.
"O ill-advised, imprudent and senseless soul,
Bear the weight of affliction but do not kill yourself.
Whether one carries the burden on the head
Or raises the head towards the skies —
When his circumstances change — in agony

81

Both will slip out of the head, in death:
Grief and pleasure do not survive, but
Good deeds and good repute are left behind —
Neither beneficence, nor crown nor throne remain.
Bestow, so that they remain from you, O auspicious one!
Do not rely on sovereignty, rank of honour or the army
Because these things were before you and will remain after you."

Sacrifice gold when ultimately you have to leave the world
Because Saadi sacrifices pearls if he does not have gold[4].

## GLOSSARY

(1)  His profession was carrying earth.
(2)  Suggests that in Saadi's day, boxing was not at all popular.
(3)  It was disfigured and the teeth had fallen out.
(4)  Through his verses.

## A STORY

They tell the story of a tyrant
Who once ruled over a country.
During his reign, day was like evening[1] for the people
Who were unable to sleep at night in terror of him.
Pious people were in distress all the time
And at night, the hands of the innocent were raised in imprecation.
A group of people came to the holy man of the time
And started weeping bitterly because of the tyrant:
"O intelligent, auspicious, ancient one!
Please tell the ruler to be afraid of God."
He replied, "I hesitate to take God's name before him
As not everyone is worthy of His message;

When you see someone rebelling against rectitude
Then, gentlemen, do not interpose the Supreme Being."

*Now, from here onwards, Saadi addresses his benefactor,*
*    Abu Bakr ibn-Saad Zangi.*
I am telling you the truth, O king of virtuous judgement;
Truths are of course given out before the pious.
I do not scatter knowledge before the ignorant —
Wasting the seeds in barren soil.
While such advice would not affect him, he would consider me an enemy,
Would be displeased and make me afflicted too.
O king, you are disciplined in rectitude
And for this reason the heart of the righteous is strong.
O well-behaved one! The engraving upon a gem
Affects wax and not the hard stone[2].
T'were not surprising if that tyrant, in his heart,
Became aggrieved: because he is a thief and I a guard.
You also are the guardian of law and justice —
May the protection of God remain upon you!
It is not in reward for your merit[3]
Because kindness, favour and thanks are due to God alone;
He has appointed you for good deeds
And has not made you idle like others.
Everyone strives on the polo field —
But not everyone wins the ball of beneficence.
You will not attain paradise through your own efforts —
God created in you the habits of the people of the abode of the blessed —
May your heart remain enlightened and satisfied!
May you remain steadfast and your rank of honour remain high!
May your life remain good and may you tread on the right path!
May your worship be accepted and your prayers granted!

## GLOSSARY

(1)  Metaphorically, the day's splendour due to the sun's light is supposed to be a delight in contrast to the darkness of the night which symbolises grief and terror.
(2)  Engravings on rings, gems etc. have their effect on wax.
(3)  If God is effecting the protection of mankind through you, it is not due to your merit but is all a bounty and kindness from God.

## DISCOURSE

For so long as the work is carried out covertly
Courtesy to the enemy is better than hostility;
When unable to subdue a foe with strength
The gate of mischief should be closed with graciousness.
If you are afraid of injury from an enemy
Keep him tongue-tied with benevolent actions.
Instead of caltrops[1], scatter gold for the adversary —
Because sharp teeth are blunted by favours.
Take advantage by stratagem and flattery —
When unable to bite it, kiss the hand.
Rustam[2] was also brought under control through ingenuity
He whose noose even Isfandyar[3] could not escape.
An opportunity should be taken to flay the enemy:
And then to treat him like a friend, with kindness.
Try to avoid conflicts with people of low standards
Because I have seen floods come from single drops —
For so long as you can, do not knit your brow.
Even if the enemy is helpless it is better to befriend him:
His enemy will be fresh and his friends wounded
Whose enemies outnumber his friends.
Do not attack an army larger in number than your own
Because the finger does not stab itself with the lancet[4].

84

f you are the stronger in battle
Remember, coercion of the weak is not valour:
Even if you have the strength of an elephant and the claws of a lion
In my opinion, peace is better than war[5].
When *all* your artifices have been frustrated
It is lawful to put your hand on your sword.
If the enemy wants peace, do not turn your face away;
If he decides to fight, do not turn the reins
Because if he will close the door of hostility
Your dignity and stature can increase a thousand-fold.
If however, he is ready to start (a war) and puts his foot in the stirrup
God will take no account from you on the day of resurrection[6].
You should also remain alert when there is sedition
Because kindness to the malicious is an error;
When you speak to any base person with grace and charm
His arrogance and pride will increase.
When the enemy enters your door with humility
Turn out the animosity and anger from your heart —
When he seeks mercy, be deedful;
Forgive him, but beware of his designs.
Do not go against the stratagems of the ancients —
Because the old are experienced;
They uproot the wall of lead from its foundation,
The young through sword and the old by intelligence
They think of a way of escape in the midst of a battle —
Do you know who was victorious
When you observe that the armies have separated?
Do not lose your precious life alone —
If you are on the sidelines try to leave;
If you are in the midst, put on the enemy's dress.
If you are a thousand strong, against two hundred-odd enemies
Do not stay in enemy territory after nightfall.
In the dark night fifty riders coming out of ambush
Scare even the earth with the pretension of five hundred soldiers.

85

If you want to travel by night
First contrive escape from attack.
When there are two armies and one marches the whole day through
Its strength and vitality is gone.
Attack a tired army with your fresh forces
Because that foolish army has committed an outrage against itself.
When you defeat the enemy do not pull down your flag
So that he should not be able to heal his wounds.
Do not pursue the fleeing for long —
You could become separated from your helpers:
In the dust of the battlefield you will see the winds as if in a mist
And then the enemies will surround you with spears and swords.
An army should not run after spoils
Leaving the king behind unguarded;
For the army the protection of the king
Is more material than plunder on the battlefield.

## GLOSSARY

(1) Caltrop = a sharp obstacle with protruding spikes, thrown in the way of horsemen.
(2) Rustam was a legendary Persian hero.
(3) Isfandyar, son of Gushtasap, was a famous wrestler. He was killed by Rustam.
(4) I.e. do not create problems for yourself.
(5) It is a Quranic saying that peace is better than war.
(6) I.e. you will not be called to account for the dead in the war.

## DISCOURSE

The hero who performs an act of valour,
According to the importance of his bravery, his rank of honour should be
    increased

Because then he will be ready to imperil his life again —
He will not be afraid of fighting against Gog[1].
Keep the army happy in time of peace
So that it may of use at a time of danger;
It is too late to kiss[2] the hands of the warriors on the battlefield
At the moment when the enemy starts beating the drums.
The soldier who does not have his equipment:
How would he be ready to die on the day of battle?
Guard the borders of the country against the evil-minded
With the army and guard the army with wealth.
The king has the upper hand over an enemy
When his troops are at ease, with their bellies full:
The soldier eats the value of his head[3].
It would not be just if he underwent hardship
If pay were withheld from the troops —
They would be reluctant to put their hands on their swords.
What valour would he display on the battlefield
Whose hands are empty and whose labour goes unrewarded?

## GLOSSARY

1) Gog and Magog, barbarians.
2) It would be merely flattery to kiss the hands of the soldiers on the eve of battle.
3) A soldier is then always ready to sacrifice his life for the country.

## DISCOURSE

Despatch a valiant person into battle against the enemy,
Send bloodthirsty lions to fight against lions,
Work in accordance with the advice of the experienced;
Because the old wolf has experience of hunting.

Do not be afraid of young swordsmen;
Be wary of the *old* and their wiles —
The youths, subduing elephants and capturing lions,
Do not know the stratagems of the old fox.
A seasoned person is intelligent
Because he has seen many ups and downs in life;
Well-bred and fortunate young men
Do not turn their heads away from the advice of their elders.
If you want to arrange your government efficiently
Do not entrust youth with the principal offices.
Do not make anyone leader
Who has not been tried in many battles.
A hound does not turn his face from a leopard
And a lion inexperienced in combat runs from a fox.
When a youth has been brought up in the hunting tradition
He will not be afraid of war.
Through wrestling, hunting, marksmanship and by ball-play
A courageous person becomes bold;
One brought up in tenderness, luxury and *hammams*
Feels anxious when he finds the gates of war open:
When two persons put him into the saddle
Even a child can throw him violently to the ground!
When you see one fleeing in battle
Kill him, if the enemy has not killed him first.
A eunuch is better than a swordsman
Who runs, turning his face away like women on the day of battle.


## A STORY

Gurgin[1] spoke well when he said to his son
As he fastened the bow and quiver into his harness,
"If you want to run away like a woman,

88

Do not go, do not vilify the name of the brave."
The rider who shows his back to the enemy in battle[2]
He spoils not only his name, but ruins the name of the brave as well.
Valour is seen when two friends
Who get involved in the circle of battle,
Two companions speaking the same language,
Fight whole-heartedly and with devotion throughout the battle.
For, it is a disgrace to save oneself from an arrow
When one's brother is held captive by the enemy.
When you see that friends are friends no longer[3]
Then consider retreat instead of looking for spoils.

## GLOSSARY

1) Gurgin was a famous Persian wrestler.
2) A soldier fleeing is the cause of the destruction of the morale of the army.
3) Because differences amongst troops lead to dissension and ultimate defeat.

## DISCOURSE

O King, protector of the weak! Patronise two types of people:
First, the strong and powerful; and secondly, the faithful.
Such people excel over the celebrated ones
Who patronise the intelligent and the swordsmen.
The one who did not practise with pen or sword
Do not say "Alas" at his death.
Take care of the writers and the swordsmen
But not the minstrel, for bravery comes not from the women:
And it is not manly when the enemy is preparing the machinery of war,
For you to be intoxicated by the beloved and the sound of the harp!
Many a prosperous people became engrossed in play
And lost their prosperity through their sport.

## DISCOURSE

I do not say that you should be afraid of war with the malicious
But rather be afraid of their messages of reconciliation;
Very many who gave signs of peace during the day;
When night fell, they marched their army upon the sleepers.
The brave sleep with the armour on
Because bedding is the night attire for ladies;
The swordsmen inside their tents
Should not sleep without their armour like women inside their houses.
Preparation for war should be made in secret
For the enemy attacks clandestinely.
Vigilance and prudence are necessary for the valiant —
The front of the army is a wall of lead[1] for the camp.

## GLOSSARY

(1)    A protective talisman.

## DISCOURSE

Between two who are both malignant and weak
It is not wise to sit at ease
Because if they were to conspire together,
Their weakness would become strength.
Keep one engaged, by deceit;
Destroy the other with his existence.
If some enemy decides to fight you
He should be slaughtered with prudence.
Go and make friends with his enemy
So that his long robe becomes a prison for him[1].

When there is dissension amongst enemy troops
You may put your sword in its sheath:
When wolves start harming each other
The sheep can live amongst them freely.
When enemy engages with enemy
Sit comfortably with your friends, with an easy heart.

## GLOSSARY

1) Long robe: metaphor for 'sense of importance.'

## A DISCOURSE IN CONNECTION WITH THE POLITE TREATMENT OF AN ENEMY AS FORESIGHT

When you draw the sword of war
Keep an eye on the way of peace;
Warriors capable of rending armies
May keep secret the pursuit of peace while openly declaring war.
Make efforts to please the valiant person's heart secretly —
Maybe he will fall at your feet like a ball:
If an enemy commander comes into your clutches
His execution should be delayed;
It is possible that one of the commanders of your troops
May get encircled somewhere:
If you had killed that wounded prisoner
You would not see your own alive again.
Are you not afraid that time may make him a prisoner
Who shows his valour on captured prisoners?
He is a protector of captives
Who has himself been held a captive.
If some commander submits to your commands

91

And you deal kindly with him, others will follow suit —
If you take ten hearts in your hand[1]
It is better than one hundred night-assaults.


## GLOSSARY

(1)  Keep at least a small number of persons happy.


# A DISCOURSE CONCERNING VIGILANCE OVER THE ENEMY
## WHO SUBMITS TO YOU

If one close to the enemy becomes your friend
Do not ever feel easy about duplicity;
Inwardly he will be wounded by ill-feeling for you
When he recollects his kinsmen's affection and love:
Do not be misled by the sweet talk of the evil-minded —
Because there may be poison in the honey.
He who would avoid trouble from the vexations of the enemy
Considers even sincere friends as aliens[1].
The artful person keeps pearls safely in the purse
Of him whom considers everybody a pickpocket!
Any soldier disobedient to his master —
If possible, do not employ him:
As he was ungrateful to his master
So he would not consider you — Beware of his treachery!
Despite sworn allegiance, do not consider him stable;
Appoint secret custodians over him.
Do not give a learner much rope
And do not cut it or you will not see him again[2].
When you capture the enemy's castle after the war
Hand it over to the prisoners

Because the prisoner dips his teeth in blood[3] —
He will suck the blood from the throat of the tyrant.
When you forcibly take possession of the country from the enemy
Keep his subjects more comfortable than he did.
If he would again knock at the door of war
The common people will break his head.
If you have made the citizens suffer hardship
Do not trouble to close the gates of the city to the enemy,
Say not that the enemy swordsman is at the city gate:
The allies of the enemy are inside the city already.
Be expedient in war with the malevolent;
Take prudent measures and keep your intentions concealed —
Do not speak your secrets before everybody
Because I have very often seen spies as pot-companions:
Sikander[4] who had planned an attack to the East —
It is said that the gate to his camp faced West;
When Bahman[5] wanted to conquer Zabulistan[6]
He spread rumours about marching to the left and started off towards the right
Let anyone other than you know your intentions
And one must deplore such lack of judgment and intelligence.
Be beneficent and desist from enmity and spite
So that you may bring the world within your grasp.
When work is done with kindness and enjoyment
What need is there to be severe and stern?
If you do not want your heart to be distressed
Have the hearts of the afflicted released from confinement.
The army does not become strong by strength of arms —
Go and get the blessings of the weak
For the blessings of weak dependants
Are more powerful than the arm of virility!
Whosoever will solicit the aid of the dervish
If even he were opposed by Faridun[7], he would win!

93

THE BOSTAN

# GLOSSARY

(1)   One who remains discreet with friends also.
(2)   The old servant is the more trustworthy.
(3)   He wades through misery and trouble.
(4)   Alexander.
(5)   A famous Persian warrior.
(6)   Zabul is a province in Persia.
(7)   Faridun was a celebrated and powerful king of Persia.

# CHAPTER TWO

## *IN CONNECTION WITH BENEFICENCE*

## IN CONNECTION WITH BENEFICENCE

If you are intelligent, look towards the realities
Because realities are more open and steadfast.
The one who does not possess either wisdom or generosity or piety[1]
Has no genuineness apparent.
He rests easy under the earth[2]
Who enabled mankind to sleep comfortably.
Think about yourself while you yet live; your own relations[3]
May not care about you dead, because of their own greed.
Spend gold and wealth now, while they are yours —
After your death they will be out of your control.
If you do not want to be disturbed in heart
Do not harden your heart against distressed people.
Distribute treasure immediately — today, whatever it is,
Because tomorrow you will not have its keys in your hands.
Take provision for the next world in your own hands[4]
Because a wife or son should not be depended upon for favours.
He wins the game of fortune in the world
Who himself lays up and takes his treasures into heaven.
With sympathy, other than the tips of my fingers[5]
Nobody massages my limbs.
Whatever you have put on the palm of your hand, do not act so[6]
That tomorrow you bite the back of your hand in repentance.
Try to hide the nakedness of the dervish[7]
So that God's veil may hide your own nakedness.
Do not turn away an indigent stranger from your door —
You may become a stranger at the doors of others:
The rich man helps the needy with their welfare
Because he fears to become a needy stranger.
Look at the condition of the heartbroken!
Might you not, one day, become heartbroken?
Make the hearts of the dejected cheerful —
Remember the days of your own helplessness.

If you are not a seeker of alms at the door of others
Then be grateful: turn not away the alms-seekers from your door.


## GLOSSARY

(1)  One with no hidden virtue is like an expressionless picture.
(2)  I.e. in the grave.
(3)  Human beings must think of their end and of the world to come, because relatives become busy after one's death and nobody cares about the dead one.
(4)  By doing good deeds, by propitiatory offerings and by distributing alms and charity, lay up treasure in heaven.
(5)  I.e. people take money from my fingers (finger-tips).
(6)  I.e. do not close the purse but distribute its contents, for God's sake.
(7)  Give clothes to the dervish to wear so that God may hide your faults.


## DISCOURSE CONCERNING THE COMFORTING OF ORPHANS AND THE SHOWING OF KINDNESS TOWARDS THEIR CONDITION

Afford shelter to the one who has lost his father[1]
Clean the dust from him and remove his thorns.
Do you not know what happened to him to make him so dejected?
A tree without roots never becomes green —
When you find an orphan with head cast down
Do not then kiss (only) your child on the cheek.
If the orphan cries who is there to bear with him his whims and airs?
If he becomes enraged who shares his load?
Take care: if he bursts into tears, the highest heaven
Trembles when an orphan cries.
With affection, dry his eyes of tears
With kindness, brush the dust from his face.
If his own shelter has left him

Rear him under your protection.
My head was the head of a crowned king at the time
When I used to put my head on the lap of my father:
If a fly alighted on my body
The minds of very many used to become perturbed.
Now if they arrest me and take me to prison
None will help from amongst my friends.
I know of the affliction of children —
Because I lost my father in childhood.

## GLOSSARY

(1) Take the orphan under your protection.

## A STORY CONCERNING THE REWARD OF BENEFICENCE

In a dream someone saw the chief of Khojand[1]
Who had once removed a thorn from the foot of an orphan;
Strolling in the garden he was saying:
"Due to that thorn how many flowers have bloomed for me?"
So long as it is possible do not abandon compassion —
When you feel pity, they will take pity on you[2].
When you become beneficent, do not be arrogant
Saying, "I am the chief and the other is inferior:"
If he is felled by the sword of time
Is not the sword of time drawn before now —
When you see thousands invoking divine favours on the state?
Thank God for his beneficence
That many people have expectations of you
While you do not expect anything from anyone.

have read that graciousness is in the nature of chiefs
That is said wrongly: it is the virtue of the prophets.

## GLOSSARY

1) Khojand is in Central Asia.
2) As the Traditions of the Prophet have it: "If you are compassionate to earthlings, the God of the Heavens will be compassionate towards you."

## A STORY CONCERNING THE VIRTUES OF PROPHETS

Once by chance no traveller
Came to the guest-house of the *Friend of Allah*[1]
His auspicious habit was not to eat in the morning
Expecting that some destitute one might be on the way.
He came out, looked in every direction
And saw near the outskirts of the valley
A lone person in the desert, lean and thin as a cane
His head and hair were white as snow from old age.
Showing kindness to him he said, "God bless you,"
And in accordance with the traditions of the generous, he bade him enter.
He said, "O pupil of my eye!
Do me the favour of accepting my salt and bread."
He replied, "Yes," rose and entered
Because he knew the Friend of Allah's custom, God's blessings be upon him.
The guardians of the Friend of Allah's guest-house
Seated the sad old man with honour —
He asked for and they arranged a cloth for serving meals
And all of them sat down.
When everyone started to speak the name of God[2]
They heard no word from the old man[3].

99

The Friend of Allah said, "O man old in years,
I do not find in you the veracity and passion usual in the old[4];
Is it not proper that at the time of eating
You take the name of the bestower of meals?
He responded, "I do not agree with you, your path is wrong:
I have followed the spiritual guide of the Zoroastrians."
The prophet of good omen understood
That the wretched old man was a Guebre[5].
He turned him out contemptuously when he saw him to be an alien
Because an unclean person looks bad amongst the chaste.
Then there was a revelation from the Glorious God
Reproaching him: "O Friend!
I gave him bread and life for a hundred years
And you hated him after such a little time.
Even if he prostrates himself before a fire
Why do you withdraw the hand of munificence?"

## GLOSSARY

(1)  *Friend of Allah* was the title given to Abraham.
(2)  Grace at meal-time: "I begin with the name of Allah, the Beneficent, the Merciful."
(3)  I.e. the old man did not take the name of God.
(4)  In old age a positive inclination towards God occurs.
(5)  Guebre = fire-worshipper.

## DISCOURSE CONCERNING BENEFICENCE TOWARDS GOOD AND EVIL PERSONS

Do not put a stop to your liberality[1]
Because there is falsehood, fabrication, cunning and fraud[2];
It is detrimental for the critic[3]

100

f he sells learning and literature for the sake of reward.
How can intelligence and law give a true verdict
When the wise man would sacrifice faith for the sake of the world?
But you buy because wiseacres
Haggle for pleasure with bargain sellers.


## GLOSSARY

(1)     Literally: Do not tie a knot to your liberality.
(2)     Do not let picking faults with others stop your munificence.
(3)     The preacher who sermonises for gain performs an evil action.


## THE STORY OF A PIOUS MAN AND A WANTON-EYED IMPOSTOR

A loquacious person came to a pious man:
"I am stuck in a bog[1];
I owe an ignoble person ten dirhams[2]
One dang of it weighs like ten maunds on my heart[3]
On his account I am in a wretched condition the whole night through.
The whole day long he is after me like my shadow;
He has vexed my heart with his language
And has inflicted as much damage to my heart as to the door[4];
Perhaps, ever since he was begotten by his mother
God did not give him anything other than those ten dirhams.
He does not know the Alif[5] of the book of religion;
He has not studied anything other than the chapter of 'what will not be
        returned'[6].
The sun has not raised its head above the mountains for a single day
On which that the shameless fellow has not knocked at my door.
I am hoping that some generous person
May give me silver to help me to get rid of the hard-hearted fellow!"

The old man of auspicious disposition listened to the speech
And put two gold coins in his sleeve[7]
The story-teller got riches
And came out of that place fresh as a sun.
One person said: "O Shaikh, do you not know who he is[8]?
Even if he dies one should not lament over him:
He is a beggar such that he would brace a saddle on a male lion[9];
He would keep a queen and knight before Abou Zaid[10]."
The pious man became troubled and asked him to keep quiet,
"You are not a man of courtesy; you should listen:[11]
If what I thought was correct[12]
I have saved his honour in public.
If he has been immodest and deceitful
Do not think that I will regret it
For I have saved my own good name and self-respect
From the hands of such a deceitful and frivolous talker."
Spend gold and silver on good and evil[13]
For it will earn goodness and ward off wrongdoing.

He is of good fortune who in the company of the wise
Learns the virtues of the pious.
If you possess intellect, judgement, prudence and discretion
You will listen to the advice of Saadi with respect
Because his discourses are of this sort
And not about eyes, curling locks of hair, the ear-lobes and a mole[14].

## GLOSSARY

(1)  Literal meaning 'entrapped in a quagmire.'
(2)  The dirham was a coin equal in weight to 3 mashas and 4 corns of barley.
     One masha = 8 rattis. 1 ratti = 8 corns of barley.
(3)  A dang is one-sixth of a dirham. A maund = approx. 82 lbs.
(4)  His speech has injured my heart as much as his demands for payment and his
     coming and going has worn out my door.

5)  In the Arabic alphabet, Alif stands for 'A'. That is to say that he does not know even the beginning.

6)  In the books of syntax and grammar, there is a chapter on words in which genders and numbers remain constant and never change.

7)  Gold coins are guineas. Thus, he gave him two guineas.

8)  Shaikh here means pious or respectable man.

9)  He is such a flatterer that he would even fasten a saddle on a lion with his talk.

10) To keep a queen and knight in chess terminology means here to mate the king with the help of the knight. Abou Zaid was a great chess player and was famous for his cunning.

11) The man advising the Shaikh.

12) I.e. if the man was indebted.

13) To spend money for a good cause is to earn goodness, and to spend money on evil things means to avoid depravity and evil.

14) Saadi's discourses do not contain romantic descriptions of things such as a beloved's eyes, her curly locks, her earlobes and the beauty of the mole on her face: all common images in Persian poetry.


# THE STORY OF A NIGGARDLY FATHER AND GENEROUS SON

One died and left a remembrance in this world:
He had an intelligent and virtuous son
Who did not close his hand like misers do, over gold
But lifted his hands from it like a liberal noble.
He would not leave the locality devoid of dervishes
And lodged travellers in his guest house;
He kept the hearts of both kinsmen and strangers happy;
Unlike his father he would not hoard gold and silver.
A man reproached him and said "O extravagant one!
Do not squander whatever you have all at once:
Goods and stock are hoarded over years —
It is not correct to throw it all away at once;
In times of destitution, you may not be able to last out
So keep in mind the reckoning during the times of abundance.

## PROVERB

How admirable the village lady's words to a girl:
'Save something during the good times against the bad;
Always keep the water-bag and the water-pot full
Because the stream does not always flow through the village.'
The life-hereafter can be gained by means of this world
The hand of the giant can be twisted by wealth
No expectation can be fulfilled empty-handed
But by means of gold you can remove the eyeballs of the white giant[1].
If you are empty-handed do not go to your friend
But if you have silver, come and bring it[2].
Do not wring empty hands before the beautiful
Because a man is nothing without wealth.
If you keep everything that you have in your hand
Then later at the time of need, your palm will be empty.
The beggars will not become stronger through your efforts[3]
But you, I am afraid, will become powerless."

### GLOSSARY

(1)   The white giant was a legendary demon killed by Rustam.
(2)   I.e. if you have gold and silver come to the house of your friend and spend it
(3)   I.e. the beggars would not become richer.

## I REVERT TO THE STORY OF A FAVOURITE SON

When the preventer of good deeds narrated this story,
The veins of the generous one became numb from modesty.
His heart became disturbed by the conversation
And he became enraged saying, "You indulge in perplexing talk!

hat which I possess
Was my ancestors' property, so my father told me.
Did not they amass it frugally?
With regrets they died and left it behind.
My father's property came into my hands —
And it will fall into the hands of my son after me.
It is better that people eat it today:
For tomorrow, after me, they would plunder it."

Eat, dress up, bestow and give relief!
Why do you preserve it from others?
Wise people take merit with themselves from the world
And the ignoble remains in his place in intense sorrow.
Give away gold and be gracious now while it is your property;
Because after you, it is out of your control.
You can do this in this world, so that you buy the next world.
Purchase, my soul, otherwise you will regret it.


## A STORY CONCERNING THE GIVING OF COMFORT TO NEIGHBOURS

Once a wife called to her husband
Not to buy bread from the street vendor:
'Go to the wheat-sellers' market
Because he is a hypocrite.
Not for customers, but on account of the swarms of flies[1]
People have not seen his face for weeks."
The husband endowed with humility, consoling her
Said to his wife "O splendour of my house, pay heed to my words —
Relying on us, he has taken up his position here:
To stop his trade would not be polite.
Follow the behaviour of the virtuous and noble —

When you are standing, take hold of the hand of the fallen,
Excuse him. For those who are truly human —
They become customers at inelegant shops[2]."

If you want to hear truth, a liberal person is the friend of God
Generosity is the tradition of the King of the Valiant, Hazrat Ali.

## GLOSSARY

(1) There are no customers at his stall — only swarms of flies.
(2) Knowing that few customers go there they think that it is better to buy there
so that the shop may at least earn something.

## A STORY

I have heard that a man on his way to the Hijaz[1]
Would pray[2] at every step he took.
So ardent and hurried was he on the way to God
That he would not pause to take the acacia thorns from his feet.
Ultimately, with such ideas distracting his mind
In his inner thoughts he admired his own efforts
Through Satan's artifices, he became puffed up with pride
That nobody could walk the way in a better manner.
If God, with Divine Mercy had not pitied him
Pride would have turned his head from the straight path.
An invisible voice from the heavens called:
"O you of good fortune and auspicious nature!
Do not be proud if you have been devout
Thinking that you have brought any present to the hall of royal audience.
The contentment of one heart by active kindness
Is better than one thousand prayers at a halting-place!"

106

## GLOSSARY

(1)  Hijaz stands here for the holy places: Mecca and Medina, in Saudi Arabia.
(2)  Saadi has used the word *Rakaat* which is a part of the prayer which includes standing, bending and prostration.

## A STORY

The wife of a king's soldier said to her husband:
"O blessed one! Get up and knock at the door of subsistence;
Go so that they may give you a share from the table
Because your children are facing hardship."
He said that the kitchen would be dead[1] that day
Because last night the king had been moved to fast.
The wife cast down her head in despair
Wounded to the heart with starvation she said to herself:
"What does the king get from fasting[2]?
Because his breaking the fast is an Eid[3] for our children!"
The one who does not fast and shows beneficence
Is better than the worldly one who abstains from food and fasts;
Fasting is acceptable for one
Who gives breakfasts to some helpless person;
Otherwise what necessity is there to suffer hardship?
Take it from yourself to eat it up yourself —
The whims of an ignorant recluse
Bring the conclusion of blasphemy and faith alike.
There is purity and clearness in water and the mirror
But the discernment of purity and clearness demand discretion[4].

## GLOSSARY

(1)  Cold, cheerless and inactive.
(2)  The fasting which causes distress to the starving is useless.

107

(3)  *Eid* is the Muslim festival which follows the fast of the month of Ramadan.
(4)  The purity and clearness of water is much better than the purity and clearness of a mirror. Viz. that worship is better from which others also get benefit.

## THE STORY OF A DESTITUTE GENEROUS PERSON AND A SUPPLICANT

A man had graciousness but no capacity
His income was not on a par with his generosity.
May God not make an ignoble person wealthy!
May the generous not suffer destitution!
He whose resolutions are too magnanimous —
His desires seldom are fulfilled[1]
Like the running flood in mountainous country[2]
This habit made the man absolutely destitute[3].
A certain destitute person wrote him a few words:
"O one with a good life and of auspicious nature!
Help me this once by giving me a little money —
Because I have been in prison these few days."
In his view nothing had any value[4]
And the generous one did not have any money in his hand.
He sent word to the enemies of the prisoner:
"In the matter of that carefree person, O people of good repute:
Take your hand from his skirt for a few days[5]
If he escapes I shall be responsible."
And from that place he went to the prison and said, "Get up
And run from this city as far as you can."
When the bird sees the cage door open
It does not have the patience to snatch breath —
He started like a zephyr from that land
So fast that the wind was unable to catch his dust.
They soon arrested the generous man:

108

'Either you bring silver or return that person."
Helpless he went to the prison
Because a bird escaped from the cage cannot be recaptured.
I heard that he was in prison for some time —
He did not cry out for help nor did he write for intercession;
For many days he did not rest or sleep at nights.
A virtuous person passing that way saw him and said:
'I do not think that you have squandered others' wealth.
How did it come about that you are in prison?"
He replied, "Yes, O blessed soul!
I did not fraudulently squander anyone's riches;
I saw a meek person hurt by confinement
And could not see his salvation but through my own confinement.
In wisdom I did not comprehend
Why I should be in comfort while the other was a prisoner."
Ultimately he died and took his renown with him —
What a wonderful life, that his name did not die!

A cheerful heart sleeping under the earth
Is better than a downhearted one living in the world.
A cheerful heart never dies —
No consequence if a cheerful-hearted body dies.


## GLOSSARY

(1)   Literally : should be entrapped. Because his intentions and desires are
      magnanimous they are seldom fulfilled/achieved.
(2)   Metaphorically the example of a generously-intentioned person is that of a
      mountain and his intentions are described as running floods.
(3)   He would spend more than his capacity.
(4)   He would have spent anything for him but he did not have the money.
(5)   The creditors should cease to pursue the prisoner.

109

## A STORY CONCERNING KINDNESS TOWARDS
## GOD'S CREATURES

A person found a thirsty dog in a desert
Panting the last breaths of its life.
The man of good conduct made a bucket of his hat to draw water —
He tied his turban to it like a rope.
He girded up his loins to try to help
And gave the feeble dog some water.
The Prophet gave news about the state of the person[1]:
"God forgave all his sins."
Beware, if you are unjust — think.
Adopt the practice of generosity and be faithful to your habit;
Not wasted was the virtue of a good action towards a dog:
How could beneficence towards a pious person be wasted?
Be generous and kind with your hands[2]
For God does not close the door of virtue to anyone.
If you do not have a well in the desert
At least put a lantern on a place of pilgrimage.
To give away a large part of your riches
Is less than giving one dinar[3] earned through labour.
Everybody carries weight according to his capability —
The leg of a locust is heavy for the ant.
O One of good disposition! Be good to all creatures
So that God does not become severe towards you tomorrow[4];
Even if you stumble, you will not be a captive[5] —
One who is the protector holds the hand of the humble.
Do not impose a burden on your subordinate
For it may be that he will become one entitled to command.
While your authority, rank and position last
Do not press the poor common man
For it could be that he will attain authority
Like the sudden queening of a pawn[6].
A man of virtuous manners following advice —

110

No heart sows the seeds of malice in him.
The barn owner does harm by feeling haughty about gleaners:
He does not apprehend that God may give riches to the needy
And puts the burden of the poor one's grief onto his own heart.
There are very many powerful ones who have fallen heavily —
And very many fallen ones have been helped by fortune.
The heart of a subordinate should not be broken
Perhaps such an oppressor himself may become a subordinate.

## GLOSSARY

(1)   According to the Traditions of the Prophet, God forgave all his sins.
(2)   Be as generous as you are able. Even if you donate a little you will be rewarded.
(3)   An ancient Arab gold coin weighing 65 grains.
(4)   On the day of resurrection.
(5)   God pardons the helper of the poor and the protector of the humble. Even if he has committed a sin, God may pardon his weakness.
(6)   The pawn is the smallest and weakest piece on a chess board whereas the queen is the strongest and the most powerful piece. On reaching the 8th rank a pawn becomes a queen in chess.

## A STORY

Because of his destitute condition, a dervish appealed
To an irascible moneyed person.
The black-hearted fellow did not give him a dinar or a dang[1];
Senselessly he shouted at him with rage.
The beggar's heart was wounded by his violence
And he raised his head from his sorrow saying, "Oh! Strange:
Why is the wealthy person sour-tempered now?
Perhaps he is not afraid of the bitterness of begging."
The short-sighted man gave orders and his servants

Turned the dervish out, chiding him with baseness
Due to ingratitude towards God.
I have heard that fortune turned its back on him —
His respectability put its foot in perdition
And the planet Mercury put pen in ink[2];
Misfortune and misery left him stark naked like garlic
So that neither furniture nor necessities remained to him nor their carrier.
Fate sprinkled him with the dust of starvation
And like a conjurer his purse and hands became empty —
His entire condition was changed.
A considerable time passed after he was ruined
And one of his slaves came into the hands of a gracious person,
Wealthy in hand and heart and splendid-minded.
Seeing any indigent being in a distressed condition
He was as happy as a poor man on seeing wealth[3].
One night a person asked at his door for a bite of food —
He walked haltingly through enduring hardships.
The kind-hearted one ordered his servant
To gratify the needs of the destitute one.
When he took a portion of food from the table
The servant cried out in an excited manner
When he returned to the master
Tears rolling down his face betrayed his agitation.
The auspicious-natured master enquired,
"Due to whose ill-treatment have tears appeared on your face?"
He replied: "My heart has become greatly disturbed
Seeing the condition of that old man in a distressed state
Because previously I was his property:
He, whose were properties, goods and chattels and silver
Has now become short of grandeur and pride
He spreads his hand begging at others' doors."
The master laughed and said, "O son, that is no tyranny.
The vicissitudes of fortune are no injustice to anybody;
Is not this the same unfortunate merchant

Who used to keep his head in the skies out of arrogance?
I am the very person whom he once had expelled from his own door —
The vicissitudes of fortune have put him in my place:
The heavens looked towards me again
And washed the dust of grief from my face.
God expediently closes some door
And opens another to show mercy and graciousness.
There are very many poor destitutes who have become sated
And the fortunes of many of the rich have been put in disarray.

## GLOSSARY

(1)  Literally: He did not give a dinar or a dang to him. These are coins: a dang
     is 1/6th of a dinar.
(2)  The planet Mercury is also called the scribe of the heavens. 'Mercury put pen
     in ink' means that fate struck out his name.
(3)  He was made happy by solving the problems of the distressed.

## A STORY

Please listen to this story about the good qualities of the virtuous
If you are a pious person of good conduct.
Shibli¹ took from the shop of a wheat seller
A bag of wheat on his shoulders to the village.
He observed that there was an ant amidst the grain
Who was running hither and thither in astonishment.
Taking mercy on it he could not sleep the whole night long —
He brought it back to its starting-place and said
"It would not be humane that the confused ant
Should be disturbed from its place of resort."
Make the hearts of the distressed tranquil
So that you have peace of mind in the world.

113

How well spoke Firdausi[2] of chaste lineage
May Divine Mercy and blessings descend on that grave!
"Do not harass the ant[3] who gnaws a single grain
Because she has life and dear life is good.
He is evil-minded and hard-hearted
Who wants to see an ant as narrow-minded."
Do not strike with powerful hand on the head of the weak
Because some day you may be trampled under his[4] feet like an ant.
The candle did not take pity on the condition of the moth;
Did you see how it guttered at the gathering?
I admit that there are very many weaker than you
But there is One who is stronger than you[5].

## GLOSSARY

(1)  Shibli was a saint. He was a disciple of Hazrat Junaid of Baghdad.
(2)  Firdausi was a famous poet at Mahmud of Ghazna's court and the author of the famous *Shahnama*.
(3)  Do not harass the weak.
(4)  Under the feet of the weak.
(5)  God Almighty.


## A MAXIM CONCERNING GENEROSITY AND ITS REWARDS

O son! Practice munificence to captivate human beings —
Through benevolent actions wild beasts are tamed.
Tie the neck of an enemy with kindness
Because that rope cannot be severed with a sword[1].
When the enemy observes generosity, kindness and munificence
Wickedness does not come into being from him again.
Do no wrong, else you will see evil from your good friends —
One does not reap a good reward from bad seeds.
If you are hard and vex your friend
He will ignore your disposition and character.

And if, O man, you have a good disposition towards your enemies
Not much time will pass ere they become your friends.

## GLOSSARY

1)   The rope of kindness.


# A STORY IN CONNECTION WITH CAPTIVATING HEARTS THROUGH BENEFICENCE

On a road I met a young man
A lamb was running and following him.
I told him that it was through imprinting
That the lamb was following him.
He immediately took off its collar and chain
And started running to the left and then the right
Just the same the lamb started following him on the way
Because it had eaten green oats and barley from his hands.
When he returned from play and sports
He saw me and said, "O Master of judgement!
Rope does not make the lamb follow me
It is beneficence that is the rope around its neck.
The kindness experienced by the mast[1] elephant
Forbids it from attacking its keeper.

O virtuous person! Be kind to bad people!
When a dog eats your bread, it guards you.
A cheetah's teeth are blunted for the person[2]
On whose cheese he rubs his tongue for a few days.


## GLOSSARY

(1)   Mast is a dangerous frenzy in some male animals such as elephants.
(2)   Cheetahs were given cheese during training.

## THE STORY OF THE DERVISH AND A FOX

A man saw a fox without hands or feet[1] —
He was amazed to see God's artifices and kindness.
How does she spend her life
With such for hands and feet; wherefrom does she eat?
The dervish was perplexed by this
When a lion appeared clutching a jackal in his paw;
The wretched jackal was eaten by the lion:
The remainder, a bellyful, was eaten by the fox.
The next day also it happened thus —
That the Giver of daily bread provided her with that day's food.
Belief opened the eyes of the dervish
He proceeded with trust in the Creator:
"After this I shall sit in a secluded spot like an ant
Because even the elephants do not eat by virtue of their strength."
For a few days he kept his chin in his collar[2]
Trusting that the Giver would by divine means send him bread.
Neither his own people nor strangers paid any attention to him
His veins, bones and skin became like a sitar[3] —
When due to weakness he lost patience and senses
From the niche of the wall came to his ears:
"O impostor! Go and become a ripping lion
Do not lie like the fox without hands and feet!
Exert yourself like a lion so that something is left over;
Why should you fill the belly with left-overs like the fox,
When your neck is stout and strong like a lion?"
If he remains like this fox even a dog were better than he.
Bring in your hands[4] and eat with the rest —
Pay no attention to others' leavings;
Eat while you can by dint of hard work
Until your attempts are in your scales[5];
Bear hardships courageously like men do and give comfort
Because only an eunuch enjoys the hard labours of others.

116

O acceptor of advice! Go and help!
Do not you throw yourself down and ask for help.
That being has God's favour
Due to whom all creation is in comfort.
The head which has brains adopts generosity
Because the spiritless people are shells without kernel.
He sees goodness in both the worlds[6]
Who transmits virtuousness to God's creation.

## GLOSSARY

(1)   The fox was crippled.
(2)   'Chin in collar' means 'in meditation'.
(3)   The sitar is an instrument like a guitar with three strings.
(4)   Literally: 'Bring in your paw' meaning 'Contribute.'
(5)   That is to say on the Day of Judgement this particular virtue will be weighed
      in a pair of scales reckoning your good and bad deeds.
(6)   In this world and in the life hereafter.

## THE STORY OF THE NIGGARDLY PIOUS PERSON

I heard that there is a person in a chaste land
He is righteous and devoted in far-off Rum[1].
I and some travellers, traversing deserts
Went to pay a visit to the pious one.
He kissed everyone's head, eyes and hands[2]
Bade us sit with dignity and respect and himself sat down;
We saw his vineyard, farm, servants, goods and chattels
But he was as ungenerous as a fruitless tree[3],
A bright person in politeness and courtesy
But his hearth was very cold.
There was no rest or sleep during the course of night

117

He, from counting beads and praising God by proclaiming[4], and we through hunger[5].
In the morning he made ready[6], opened the door,
And started again the courtesies of the previous night.
There was a sweet and witty person of cheerful disposition
Who was in that country in the house with us.
He said, "Kiss us with Tasheef[7]
For provisions are better for the dervish than a kiss;
Do not put your hands on my shoes to pay me homage
Give me bread and hit me on the head with shoes."
People have won merit by dint of practising selflessness;
People awake all night for prayers are not exhausted.
I saw the same thing in a watchman of Tatar[8] —
Exhausted, yet with eyes open throughout the night.
Respectability lies in generosity and in giving bread —
Idle discourses are an empty drum.
He will be in paradise on the Day of Judgement
Who sought truth and abstained from laying claim to greatness.
Claims of greatness can be correct when inwardly one has become right
Talk with no foundation is a very weak support.

## GLOSSARY

(1)   Rum is Asia Minor.
(2)   In parts of the East it is the custom that the elder person kisses the head, eyes and hands of the younger visitor.
(3)   He was rich but miserly.
(4)   Here the word used by Saadi is *Tahleel* which means proclamation of "There is no God but the One God".
(5)   He did not give us anything to eat and all of us were hungry.
(6)   In the Persian text: 'he girded his loins'.
(7)   In the Persian script any change of points (*Nuqtas*) and reading one as another word with changed meanings is called *Tasheef*. Here the word for kiss is *Bosa*. Now the B of the Bosa has a point (*Nuqta*) below it, if it is changed into two points (*Nuqtas*) and placed above the B it would read *Tosha* which means 'provisions'.
(8)   Tatar is an area of Turkestan.

118

## HATIM TAI AND HOW HE EXCELLED IN LIBERALITY

have heard that in the days of Hatim[1]
here was a fleet-footed fumy horse in his stable[2]
A bay, swift as a zephyr, with a thunderous neigh
Who would outrun even the lightning
His galloping sounding as if a hail-storm had come to the mountains and
    the deserts[3];
You would say that a spring cloud had passed —
Traversing deserts like a torrent
Even the winds would fly about like dust behind him.
Persons endowed with knowledge said these things
As they narrated Hatim's anecdotes to the king of Rum[4]:
'He has no peer in liberality
There is no horse like his horse in speed or in war;
It traverses the desert like a boat crossing the water —
Even a crow would not fly faster."
Thus spoke the king to his intelligent vizier:
To make a boast of it is definitely to suffer shame —
will ask for that Arabian horse from Hatim Tai
And if he favours the request and gives way
Then I will know that he has grandeur;
And if he refuses, these are but empty drums[5]."
A sensible messenger fully conversant with Tay[6]
Was sent accompanied by ten others.
The earth was dead and the clouds were mourning over it —
The easterly wind put life into it[7].
They reached their destination, Hatim
And were refreshed as one thirsty on the banks of Zend Rod[8] —
He spread a table cloth and slaughtered a horse,
Gave them sugar in their skirts and handfuls of gold[9];
The night they stayed there and the next day
The messenger said what he had been briefed to say —
He was talking and Hatim was perplexed. Like, a deranged person

In intense sorrow he went to cut his hand with his teeth[10]:
"O, fortunate, renowned and wise person
Why did you not give me this message earlier?
I, of the swift running horse[11] speedy as the wind,
Gave you the roasted meat last night!
I knew that on account of rain and flooding
It would not be possible to go to the horses' grazing-grounds —
My attention and way was not to any other end —
Besides, I did not have another one in these, my camping-grounds[12].
According to my custom and usage I did not think it polite
That guests sleep with a sore heart due to hunger[13]:
I need obvious renown in the world
Though there be no famous thing to ride upon."
He gave them robes of honour, horses and money:
Good manners are innate and are not acquired by labour.
The news of Tay's munificence reached Rum;
They commended his nature a thousandfold.

Do not be happy only over the short story of Hatim
Listen to a more wonderful incident.


## GLOSSARY

(1)  Hatim was the son of Abdellah ibn-Saad of the Tay tribe. He was famou
     for his munificence.
(2)  Literally : swift like smoke.
(3)  Running at speed his hooves made such an uniform noise that it felt as if hai
     was falling.
(4)  Rum = Asia Minor.
(5)  Empty drums = claims of generosity.
(6)  Tay was the name of the tribe of Hatim.
(7)  It was the rainy season.
(8)  Zend Rod is a famous river near Isfahan with clear waters.
(9)  That is to say that he entertained them to their satisfaction.

0) In Persian literature, in perplexity of mind one bites the hand with one's teeth in regret.
1) Literally, the word here is *Duldul* which was a famous, fast mule presented by the Prophet to his cousin and son-in-law, Hazrat Ali.
2) Another horse.
3) I.e. I did not want you to remain hungry.


## THE STORY OF THE TRIAL OF HATIM BY THE KING OF YEMEN

do not remember who told me this story:
here was a king in Yemen
ho had excelled the celebrated in riches —
e had none equal to him in bestowing treasures;
e can be described as a cloud of beneficence
ecause his hands used to shower dirhams¹ like rain.
obody used Hatim's name before him
ithout him becoming enraged,
For how will you talk about this wretch —
ho has no country, no treasure nor is he entitled to command?"
heard that he held a majestic festival,
atronised the public like a harp². Someone mentioned Hatim —
nother started admiring him;
alousy turned into enmity in the being of the king:
e assigned a person to assassinate him.
For, as long as Hatim is present during my reign
shall not enjoy good renown."
he seeker of evil took his way to Bani Tay³
o accomplish the murder of the generous one.
young man welcomed him on the way
rom whom he scented sincerity;
andsome, intelligent and pleasant-tongued
e took him that night as his guest

And showed him kindness, sympathised with him and apologised[4] —
With his goodness he captured the heart of the malevolent one:
In the morning he kissed his hands and feet
And requested him to stay a few more days.
"No, I cannot stay
Because there is an important affair at hand," he said,
"If you will keep it between ourselves
I will make efforts to repay you with my life like congenial friends."
He went on, "Listen, O brave person! And pay attention —
Because I know that the splendid keep secrets.
Perhaps you know Hatim in this land
Who has a blessed name and is well-mannered.
The king of Yemen has asked for his head —
I do not know what the reason is for the enmity between them.
Can you guide me to the place where he is
My friend; I hope for this after your kindness."
The young man laughed and said, "I am Hatim.
The head is present, disjoin it from my body with the help of the sword
It is not expedient that when it is daybreak
You come to harm and are disappointed."
When Hatim held his head down for the stroke
A scream came out of the young man.
He fell down to the ground and then got to his feet
Sometimes kissing the earth, sometimes the other's hands and feet.
He threw away the sword and put down his quiver
Kept his hands on his chest like an obedient servant:
"If I hit your person even with a flower
I am not a man, but in the eyes of men I am a woman!"
He kissed his eyes and embraced him —
And from there made his way back to Yemen.
The king, looking between the eyebrows of the person
Immediately perceived that he had not accomplished the task.
He said, "Come, what is the news with you?
Why did you not tie the head to the saddle-straps?

erhaps that man of renown attacked you
nd you did not have the endurance for the fight, due to weakness."
he clever young man kissed the earth
raised the king and paid him homage
aid to him, "O generous and understanding king!
isten to the tale of Hatim:
found the renowned Hatim
killful, of excellent countenance, and handsome:
found him brave and intelligent
1 bravery, I found him superior to me —
lis favours and kindness doubled my back[5]
Ie killed me with the sword of kindness and grace!"
hen he described whatever favours he had been shown.
he king praised the people of Tay —
he person sent was rewarded with gold coins and money
o put a seal on the name of Hatim with kindness.
Ie has the right if people bear witness
hat fact and his reputation should go together.

## GLOSSARY

1) Dirhams = coins.
2) As people become happy with the sound of the harp, the king made them happy.
3) Bani (sons of) Tay was the name of Hatim's tribe.
4) Apologised for any deficiencies in entertainment.
5) 'Doubled my back' means to become so overburdened on account of kindnesses and favours as to become almost a hunchback.

123

# THE STORY OF HATIM'S DAUGHTER DURING THE TIMES OF THE PROPHET

I have heard that Tay, during the time of the Prophet[1]
Did not accept the decree to adopt the religion[2]:
An army was sent as messengers of the good news and to intimidate them[3]
The army arrested a few of their company —
Orders were given that the hated ones be put to the sword
As they were fearless and belonged to an unclean religion[4].
A woman said, "I am the daughter of Hatim.
I implore from this famous commander —
O respected one — afford clemency to me!
For my father was one of a charitable nature!"
On orders from the Holy Prophet
Her hands and feet were unfettered.
They drew sword amongst the rest of the tribe
Spilling blood ungrudgingly.
Crying, the woman then humbly entreated the executioner,
"I should be executed with the rest —
I do not merit any benevolence, any liberation from arrest
That I should remain relieved and my companions remain under duress."
Thus she spoke, crying over her brethren of Tay
And her voice came to the ears of the Prophet —
The tribe was forgiven and she was also rewarded
Because neither lineage nor a gem ever commit an error[5].

## GLOSSARY

(1)   Tay was the name of the tribe of Hatim, the most generous person ever known.
(2)   They did not accept Islam as their religion and were not afraid of God.
(3)   Literally in the Persian text *Bashir and Nazir* — which means: good tidings of paradise on conversion to Islam and, in case of non-acceptance, advice about the sufferings, pain and punishment they would receive on the Day of Resurrection.

4)   They were not afraid of God.
5)   Lineage or the stock of the person can never remain a secret. Like the jewel
     which shines even in the dark, the essence gives its scent to all and in any
     place, under every circumstance. Here it means that the good tribe of Tay would
     not be treacherous; and the woman was indeed the daughter of Hatim.


## A STORY OF LIBERALITY AND HATIM IN CONNECTION WITH THE KING OF ISLAM[1]

From the camp of Hatim an old man
Asked for ten dirhams of sugar[2] —
   remember this —
That he sent a sack of sugar out to him.
A woman from the tent asked about this policy:
The requirement of the old man had been for ten dirhams.
The celebrity of Tay heard these words[3]
And laughed saying, "O comfort of the heart of Hay![4]
Although he made his request according to his need:
What about the magnanimity of the progeny of Hatim?"

A liberal person, like Hatim, will
Not be born in these later times, but
Abu Bakr ibn-Saad whose hand of kindness[5]
Has the liberality to close the mouth of the petitioner:
'O protector of subjects! May your heart remain happy —
May the Muslim faith flourish due to your efforts!
The dust of this auspicious land takes pride
In your justice in the lands of Greece and Rum[6] —
Like Hatim who, if there had been no renown
Nobody in the world would have mentioned the name of Tay —
Only eulogy remains in the books of the celebrated.
Your praise and reward will also remain
Because Hatim sought renown and reputation —

125

Your endeavours and labour are for the sake of God.
There is no formality with this dervish-like person
There is no precept more than this one saying:
In your efforts struggle as hard as you can for goodness —
Your piety will remain — and the speech from Saadi[7].

## GLOSSARY

(1) Abu Bakr ibn-Saad Zangi, a famous Persian king.
(2) 1 dirham = 2/3 of an attic drachm.
(3) Tay was the name of the tribe of Hatim.
(4) Hay was the name of the tribe of Hatim's wife.
(5) I.e. the hand of Abu Bakr Saad was so liberal that it used to fill the mouth of the seeker.
(6) Rum = Asia Minor.
(7) I.e. Saadi speaks without formality.

## A STORY CONCERNING THE PRACTICE OF FORBEARANCE BY KINGS

A man's donkey became bogged down in mud
Blood came to his heart through passion;
What with the jungle, rain, cold weather, flowing water
And darkness spreading its skirt on the surroundings
He spent the whole night until morning in a frenzy
Shouting absurdities, imprecations and curses.
His tongue spared neither enemy nor friend
Nor the king, because that jungle and land was his.
As God would have it, the celebrated king of that land
Was in the hunting ground with polo sticks and balls
And heard those wild words
Which he did not have the patience to hear, nor any occasion to reply.

126

he man glanced and saw that the king of the land
ad heard the words from the hillock.
he king looked towards the train of his servants confusedly:
Why is he mad with rage at me ?"
)ne said, "O king! Kill him with the sword
ecause he has spared none; not their daughters nor their wives!"
he king, magnanimous in dignity, observed the man:
aw him in his affliction with his donkey in the mire,
ardoned the wretched person
uppressing his anger over the vilificatory language.
le gave him money, a horse, a long robe and fur garments —
low fair does kindness look in the face of anger.
. man said, "O old, stupid and indiscreet person,
low wonderful that you escaped execution!" He replied, "Be silent:
? I lamented over my affliction
le rewarded me at once, according to his own dignity."

o reward evil with evil is not difficult
? you are human be benevolent to a doer of evil deeds.


## THE STORY OF A MEAN-SPIRITED RICH PERSON
## AND A DERVISH

have heard that a haughty person, intoxicated with pride
:losed the door of his house on a mendicant.
hat fellow grew tired and sat down in a corner
Vith warm liver and deep sighs from a burning heart[1].
\ blind person heard him
\nd asked, "What involved you in fervour and anger?"
le explained and started weeping onto the dust of the street
?rom the injustice visited on him by that haughty person.
he blind one said, "O Sir! Forget the woe!

127

Tonight, please break your fast with me."
With virtue and prudence he pulled at his collar[2],
Brought him home and laid down a tablecloth.
The enlightened dervish had ample food
Blessed him, and implored that God grant him eyesight.
In the night a few drops fell from his narcissus[3] —
In the morning he opened his eyes and saw the world.
This story spread around the town and there was excitement
That the previous night a blind person had gained his sight.
The hard-hearted man heard the tale
He, whose illiberality had turned the dervish away:
He said, "O fortunate one! Tell me
How this difficulty became easy for you?
Who lighted these world-illumining candles for you?"
He said, "O tyrant of wretched times!
You were short-sighted and so slothful in judgement
That you entangled yourself with an owl instead of Huma[4].
He it is who opened the door for me
He on whose face you had closed the door.
If you will kiss the ashes of your great ones[5]
By the great ones you will achieve the splendour before you;
Those who are blind at heart —
It is they who are ignorant of this panacea!"
When the one with adverse fortune heard this reproach
Out of grief he bit his finger —
"My royal falcon got entangled in your snares
This wealth was mine and it was put in your name."

How can he catch hold of a falcon
Who like a mouse has sunk his teeth in greed.

## GLOSSARY

(1)  'A warm liver' stands for grief.
(2)  Humbly and politely he took him home.

3) Narcissus = eyes.
4) The *Huma* is a legendary bird. It is said that whosoever comes under the shadow of the Huma's wings becomes a king.
5) The ashes of the saints.


## A MAXIM FOR THE CONSOLATION OF CREATURES TO HELP THEM TO REACH SOME GENEROUS PERSON

Be warned if you are a seeker of the devout:
Do not be negligent, even for a moment failing to pay attention —
Offer grains to partridges, quails and pigeons
So that one day the Huma may fall into your trap.
When you shoot arrows of humility to all sides
It is to be expected that you will catch something someday;
A pearl comes from hundreds of oysters
Out of a hundred arrows, one will find its mark.


## A STORY IN THIS CONTEXT

A man's son went missing at a halt:
He searched for him through the night among the caravans
Enquired at every tent and ran in all directions
And in the dark he found his son.
When he approached the people of a caravan
I heard him saying to the camel driver:
"You do not know how I reached the friend —
Whosoever came before me I said, 'It is he[1].'"
Holy are the seekers of every person through their inwardness
It may be that they find the sought-after one sometime:
They endure too much for the sake of one heart[2]
Are pricked by many thorns for the sake of one flower.

## GLOSSARY

(1) He enquired of everyone, taking him to be his son, until he ultimately foun‹ his son.
(2) In their search they serve very many people before achieving their goal.

## ANOTHER STORY IN THIS CONTEXT

From the crown of a prince in the camp
A ruby fell to the stony ground.
In the dark his father asked him,
"How do you know which is a gem and which a pebble?
O son! Look at all the stones —
The ruby will not be other than one of them!"
Distracted, virtuous people in the midst of sceptics
Are rubies and stones in a very dark place.
Bear the burden of every uncultured person with honour
One day you will come upon some holy one.
If one is in love with his sweetheart
Do you not see how he endures the burden of an enemy?[1]
His clothes torn like flowers by the thorns
With heart immersed in blood, yet he laughs like a pomegranate[2].
In the cause of love for one, suffer grief from very many —
For the sake of one, afford privileges to one hundred.
If the fallen and the mad
Are contemptible and abject in your eyes —
Then you do not look at them with approval at all
Because their being the favoured of God is sufficient.
Any person who, in your opinion, is bad
May be a saintly person, unbeknownst to you;
The doors of the knowledge of God are open for those
To whom the doors of their fellows are closed;

Very many with lives harsh who have tasted bitterness
Will come with skirts gathered, attired in elegant clothes[3].
If you have intellect and prudence, kiss
The hands of the prince in prison[4] —
For, one day, he will be released;
He will raise you up when he is exalted.
Do not burn the perennial trees in the autumn
Because at the dawn of spring they will look fresh (again).

## GLOSSARY

(1)   For the sake of the beloved, one has to bear the rivals.
(2)   Literally: he whose heart is in blood due to love, he laughs like a pomegranate. The metaphor here arises because when the seeds of a pomegranate ripen, its leathery rind bursts open exposing the seeds and giving the impression that it is laughing.
(3)   Those who have suffered misfortunes, calamities and miseries in worldly life will be dressed in elegant clothes in paradise.
(4)   When they are reprimanded be kind to them so that on attaining power they favour you.

## THE STORY OF A NIGGARDLY FATHER AND A RECKLESS SON

A man did not have the desire to spend
He had money and property but did not have the spirit to consume:
Neither would he eat to afford himself comfort
Nor would he donate that it might be of use on the Day of Resurrection.
Day and night he was always thinking about gold and silver —
Gold and silver was imprisoned by a sordid person.
One day the son looking from a hidden place
Saw where the miser had put it under the earth.
He took it out and squandered it —
I have heard that he placed a stone there.
Gold did not last with the young man

It came to him with one hand and he squandered it with the other:
He was so prodigal and ill-mannered
That his cap and tunic were always pawned in the market.
The father started wailing and lamentations —
The son called the guitar and clarion players[1].
The father did not sleep the whole night with crying and lamenting;
In the morning the son laughed and said,
"O father, gold is for spending —
For hoarding gold and stone are alike;
Gold is mined from the hard stone
So that when it is bestowed, one can dress up and eat comfortably."
Gold kept in the palm of the hand of a person of the world
Might as well be still inside the stone.
When you are not fair with your children in your lifetime
And they wish for your death — do not complain of it;
You are like a scare-crow — they will feast when
You fall down from a precipice fifty yards high.
A rich miser in possession of sovereigns and silver
Is like a magic spell standing guard over treasure[2];
It is for this that his money is hoarded for years
So that such a spell guards his head:
With the stone of death they will break it suddenly
And with contentment they will divide the treasures between them.
After taking it away and collecting like an ant
Eat it before the insects of the grave eat you.
Saadi's words are metaphorical maxims
They will be of use to you if you practice them;
It is regrettable to disregard them —
Through them one can find prosperity.

# GLOSSARY

(1)  Literally: the father put the guitar in his mouth. This means that he started

1)   wailing and crying. (It is quite a free translation.) When 'the son called the guitar and clarion players' it means that he started mimicking his father.
2)   It is said that the image of a snake is put above treasures and then magic spells are woven so that the snake looks like a python to whosoever disturbs the treasure.

# A STORY CONCERNING A SMALL BENEVOLENT ACTION AND ITS LIMITLESS REWARD

A young man had donated a dang[1]
And fulfilled the request of an old man.
Suddenly, out of the blue, they arrested him for some crime —
The king sent him to the place of execution;
Spectators were watching from doorsteps, streets and roof-tops
The parading of the soldiers and the excitement of the populace.
When the old dervish saw in the midst of that tumult
The young man under arrest by the authorities
His heart grieved for the poor fellow
Because he had once comforted him.
He started shrieking and shouted, "The king is dead;
The world remains and he has taken his good habits away with him"
And he wrung his hands in regret.
The soldiers with swords drawn heard this —
Their wailing started an uproar:
Lamenting and beating their faces, heads and shoulders
Up to the gate of the palace of audience fleetly
They ran and saw the king on the throne.
The young man escaped from their midst and they arrested the old man
Dragged him by the neck to the throne of the king as a prisoner.
They threatened him and asked him and overawed him:
"What was the reason that you wanted me dead
When my habits are good and correct —
Why did you become malignant towards mankind[2]?"

133

The bold old man unloosed his tongue,
"O King, may the world remain your subject!
That false rumour that the king was dead
Did not make you die but the poor fellow did save his skin."
The king was so pleased with the story
That he rewarded him and did not remonstrate with him.
For his part the young man who had been in difficulty
Was running to and fro:
On the square of retaliation[3] one asked him,
"What did you do to get released?"
He whispered to him, "O man of good sense,
For one life and one dang I went free[4]."
One sows a seed in the soil for the purpose
That on the day of need it fructifies —
An ear of barley wards off misfortune.
Did not you see that Auj was killed by an ordinary stick?[5]
After all, the saying of the Prophet is correct —
Favour and kindness ward off evil;
You will not see the feet of the enemy in this country
For Abu Bakr Saad is the king.
O King! The world is happy with your face, take
Another world and may God keep your face happy.[6]
In your reign no one was oppressed by any,
In the garden the flower did not endure the cruelty of thorns;
You are the shadow of God's favours on earth —
Like the prophet you are the divine blessing for both the worlds.
Of what concern is it if someone does not know your rank of honour –
People do not know even the Shab-e-Qadr[7].

## GLOSSARY

(1)   A dang is 1/6th of a dirham.
(2)   Wishing for the death of a good king is considered malignant.

3) Criminals used to be executed on this square as an example to the people.
4) Literally : I got saved on account of one person and one dang.
5) Ordinary propitiatory offerings ward off big misfortunes. The staff of Moses finished off Auj Bin Anaq. He was a legendary tall being, 3500 years of age. He was so tall that the deluge of Noah reached his back only. He would catch a fish from the sea, roast it in the sun and eat it. Yet Moses killed him with his ordinary staff.
6) Acquire the next world.
7) The 27th night of Ramadan — the date on which the Quran began to be revealed.


## FRUIT OF GOODNESS

Someone saw the doomsday square in a dream —
The face of the earth was like hot copper in the sun
The clamour and noise of men reached heaven
The brain was boiling in the heat.
In the midst of all one person was in the shade
The cloak of paradise about his neck.
Someone asked, "O elegance of the assembly,
Who was your helper in this multitude?"
He replied, "There was a vine at the gate of my house
A pious person was sleeping in its shadow,
That virtuous man in this hour of trial
Besought the Just Ruler about my sins:
'O God forgive this humble servant
For I have found comfort from him for a while.'"

When I solved this mystery, I was delighted —
These are glad tidings for the king of Shiraz
Because the world remains in the shelter of his magnanimity
And surrounded by his blessings and favours.
A liberal person is a fruit-bearing tree
And anything apart from that is fuel and firewood;

If we axe the root of a firewood tree
When do we cut down the fruit-bearing tree?
"O tree of virtue, may God make you durable
Because you are fruit-bearing as well as shady."


## THE KING'S DREAD AND A PROVERB ABOUT THE POLITICS OF THE COUNTRY

We have said much about beneficence
But it is something that is not expedient for all.
Drink the blood and eat the property of people who harass mankind
For it is better for the vicious bird to have its feathers and quills plucked
Whosoever has a fight with your master[1]
Why do you put a stick and stone in his hand?
Extirpate the root which grows thorns
Nourish the tree which yields fruits
Give the rank of honour of chief to him
Who does not show peevishness to subordinates
Do not forgive wheresoever there is one who is cruel
Because to take pity on him is cruelty to the world —
The extinguishing of the lamp of the cruel is better:
One getting burned is better than for all to suffer.
When you seek to take pity on the thief
With your strength you are robbing the caravan.
Exterminate the oppressors —
Acts of cruelty towards oppressors are justice and fair play.


## GLOSSARY

(1)   A wicked person is an enemy of God. He should not be helped.


136

## A PROVERB CONCERNING A PERSON WHO DOES
## NOT DESERVE AN ACT OF KINDNESS

heard that someone was worried about his house
Because wasps had made a nest in his roof.
His wife asked, "What concern is it of yours? Do not exterminate them
Because it would be dislodging the poor from their dwelling:
The stupid husband got absorbed in his work
Until one day the wasps stung the wife.
When the husband returned to his house from the shop
The stupid wife was very angry with him
She, in the door of the upper storey and on the street,
Was shouting and the husband said,
'O woman do not pull faces for others to see:
You told me not to kill the poor wasps."
How can one do good to unworthy persons —
Toleration of the wicked increases the mischief[1].
f you see trouble in another's mind
Vex his throat with a sharp sword.
What is a dog that people should lay a place at table for him?
Give orders so that they give him a bone.
How aptly the old man of the village said,
'It is better to load the donkey which is kicking its hind legs[2]."
f the soldier shows magnanimity
Nobody would be able to sleep for fear of thieves.
On the battle-field the point of a spear
s a hundred thousand times more valuable than sugarcane.
Not everybody deserves wealth —
One wants goods, the other needs chastisement.
When you go to caress the cat she will seize the pigeon;
When you fatten the wolf he will maul Joseph[3].
The building which has no strong foundations —
Raise it no higher — if you do, be careful[4].

## GLOSSARY

(1)　It is not advisable to connive at mischief, specially with unworthy persons. They tend to take advantage thinking that the other party is weak.
(2)　A loaded donkey does not kick.
(3)　The patriarch Joseph, son of Jacob.
(4)　Do not give latitude to the base person, and if indeed you are lenient with him be careful of him.

## CONSIDERATION OF FORESIGHT AND ITS RESULT

How shrewd the words of Bahram, the hermit of the desert[1]
When a headstrong horse threw him to the ground violently:
Another foal should be taken from the herd
Which could be nurtured while it is restive.
The source of a spring should be closed by a needle —
When it is full-sized it would not be possible to cross even on elephant-back.
O son! put up an embankment when the Tigris is receding
For when it is flooding it would be of no use.
When a malignant wolf comes into your noose
Kill him or cease to grieve for the sheep.
Satan never prostrates himself before God
Neither does any virtue come from any base one.
Do not give any quarter or occasion for mischief to the evil-minded —
The enemy is better lodged in a well and the monster in a bottle.
Do not say that this snake must be killed with a stick:
When he puts his head under your stone, hammer him!
The scribe who has done wrong to a defenceless person
It is better to cut off his hand with a sword.
The minister who promotes a bad law —
He is taking you to hell;
Do not say that this minister is meet for the country —
Do not call him a manager because he is a wretched person.

. well-disposed person complies with Saadi's sayings
ecause that is in the interest of the country and they embody prudence and
idgement.

## GLOSSARY

.) Because Bahram was very fond of hunting wild asses he would pass most of his time in the desert — hence he is called the hermit of the desert.

# CHAPTER THREE

## *IN CONNECTION WITH LOVE*

## IN CONNECTION WITH LOVE

The time of persons 'desperately in love with God' passes happily
Whether they are at one or are afflicted by separation[1].
They are such beggars that sovereignty is repugnant to them —
In longing for Him they are patient in their mendicancy.
They drink the wine of grief incessantly
Even if they feel bitter, they are quiet and without complaint.
In the pleasure of wine there is the hangover[2];
On the stem of the flower the thorn is armed and equipped;
Patience in remembrance of Him is not bitter
Because bitterness from the hands of the Friend is sweet.
His captive does not seek liberty from bondage,
His prey does not seek liberty from the lasso.
God's mendicants are the kings of seclusion
If their steps cannot be retraced, they know the goal —
Frenzied lovers tolerant of reproaches.
The excited camel carries the burden swiftly —
When do the created come to know about their path
For, like the spring of the water of immortality, they are in the dark[3].
Like the Holy House their innermost part is full of splendour[4]
The external walls have been left dilapidated and ruined;
Like the moth they throw themselves into flames —
They do not practise self-decoration like the silkworm.
Seekers of the Most High God have their Beloved in their embrace[5]
They are on the bank of the river with lips parched by thirst:
I do not say that they have no power over water
But they are as dropsy patients on the banks of the Nile.

## GLOSSARY

(1)  Union or connection with God.
(2)  Sickness is caused by the effects of intoxication so that not every greedy person
     does start drinking.

3) Just as finding the fabulous spring containing the water of immortality is difficult because it is in the dark, so it is difficult to find a pious and godly elder.
4) The temple at Jerusalem.
5) In spite of connection with the sweetheart their desire does not become subdued.


# A DISCOURSE COMPARING THE STABILITY OF TRUE LOVE WITH INSTANCES DEMONSTRATING EXAGGERATED EARTHLY LOVE

Your being in love with one made of clay and water like you
Makes patience and ease of heart disappear.
In wakefulness enamoured of her features,
Keeping her image in mind when asleep —
You put your head at her feet so ardently
That in the face of her existence you sense the world as non-existent
And when the sweetheart disregards your wealth
Then gold and clay look alike to you.
Then your heart is not charmed by anyone else
Because in her presence there is no room for any other.
You would say that her abode is in the eyes
And if you close your eyes she is in your heart[1].
You are not afraid of being disgraced by anyone
Nor have you the capacity to become patient suddenly.
If she asked for your life, you would give it into the palm of her hand
And if she put a sword to your head you would bend your neck.
This love, the foundations of which are carnal
Is so seditious and commanding —
And yet you are surprised at the devotees of the Path[2]
Who are immersed in the ocean of reality,
Who in thinking of the Beloved[3] are careless of their lives,
And unmindful of the world in reciting praises of the Beloved;
In recollection of God they have shunned the created,

143

So intoxicated with the love of the Beloved One are they that they have
  spilled the wine.
It is not proper to cure them with medical treatment
Because no one has diagnosed their ailment.
From the beginning ALAST is ringing in their ears[4]
They clamour and cry out for help
A group of workers are recluses[5] —
Their feet are soiled and their breath is fiery:
With one slogan they could remove a mountain from its place
With one sigh they could ravage the country.
Invisible as the wind and swift[6]
They are soft like musk and are ever in the act of praising God;
They weep so much at the close of night that tears
Wash the collyrium of sleep from their eyes;
Their horse is dying as it has been ridden too much in the night[7]
Asking for succour — in the morning they are distressed;
Day and night they spend in the ocean of impulsive passion
Due to their frenzy they cannot discriminate between night and day[8].
They have fallen so in love with the Painter[3]
That the beauty of form and appearance are of no concern to them
The pious do not fall in love with skin[9]
And if any stupid one has done so, he is a blockhead and ignorant.

He is intoxicated with the pure wine of the Oneness of God[10]
Who has relinquished this world and the world hereafter.


## GLOSSARY

(1)  In wakefulness the sweetheart is accommodated in your eyes and during sleep
     it is she who comes into your dreams.
(2)  When this is the condition in earthly love, why should one feel surprised at
     conditions prevailing in real love?
(3)  God.

144

(4)   In the Traditions, God assembled all the spirits on the Day of Genesis and enquired from them: "ALAST BE RUBBEKUM?" meaning, "Art thou not My Creature?" upon which all of them replied: "BALA" meaning, "Verily it is Thou". That is called the times of ALAST.

(5)   Saints. *Abdal* and *Aqtab* are the names of ranks amongst religious mendicants. They have been appointed for creative and constructive tasks.

(6)   They are hidden from the eyes of the worldly but they are beneficent ones.

(7)   'Horse' here signifies the human body. Praying the whole night they become tired and distressed but in the morning they again become impatient and restless and say that their destination is still far away.

(8)   That is to say that days and nights are the same to them.

(9)   The chaste and pious do not heed the form, appearance and complexion of the skin which are all worldly things.

(10)  *Wahdat*: the Oneness of Godhead.


# THE STORY OF A BEGGAR'S SON AND A PRINCE

I heard once that a beggar's son
Fell in love with a prince.
He went about cherishing his vain hopes —
His vision was to attain the object of his desire[1]:
He was like a goal-post in the playground[2]
Always remaining like a bishop by the side of the knight[3].
His heart became sore and the secret remained within
But his feet were bogged down in the mire through weeping[4]:
The guards came to know of his secret.
They said, "Do not wander about here again."
He left for a little while but remembering the face of the friend
He again encamped in the street of the friend
And a slave broke his head, his hands and his feet.
"Did we not tell you not to come here again?"
Again he went away, but he had neither patience nor repose —
Unable not to see the friend's face.
Though he was removed, like a fly from sugar

Soon he would reappear.
Someone told him, "You barefaced lunatic!
It is surprising that you tolerate sticks and stones."
He said, "This cruelty to me is from him[5]
And it is not becoming to complain of treatment at the hands of the friend.
I am practising friendship now
Whether he regards me a friend or a foe.
In his absence do not maintain an expectation of self-restraint from me
Because even in his presence there is no possibility of repose for me[6]:
I do not have the strength to endure nor can I contend
I do not have the possibility to stay, nor the feet with which to escape.
Do not say that I turned away my head from this palace of audience
Even if he secures my head like a nail to the tent.
The moth, sacrificing his life under the feet of the friend,
Is better than a moth alive in a dark corner."
"Suppose you are wounded by his polo-stick?"
He replied, "Then I will fall down at his feet like a polo-ball."
"What if he severed your head with the sword?"
His response was, "I would not regret it —
When someone has a sole beloved
He does not become angry with him over petty things
I do not have any intimation from my head
Whether there is a crown over it or an axe.
Do not be angry with me for my impatience
Because in love there is no aspect of patience!
Even if I become blind like Jacob[7]
Even then I would not give up the expectation of seeing Joseph."
One day the young man kissed the prince's stirrup —
He became enraged and pulled the reins, turning away from him.
He laughed and said, "Do not pull at the reins
Because the king's attention never turns to something else[8].
I am a non-entity before your existence
In thinking of you I lost my self-conceit
Even if you see my faults, do not wound me —

It is you who has taken his head from the garments of my breast[9].
I mustered the courage to put my hand on your stirrup
Because I do not take myself into account[10].
I have drawn a line through my name
And trodden on my scope and desires;
The arrow from those intoxicating eyes could kill me[11]
What need is there to draw the sword?
You set the brush on fire and go away
So that neither the withered nor the green remains in the jungle.

## GLOSSARY

(1)   Literally: His vision had put its teeth into its objective.
(2)   He was always to be found on the playground.
(3)   The reference here is to two chess pieces. Before the commencement of the game the bishop and the knight are side by side.
(4)   His weeping disclosed the secret of his love.
(5)   I.e. when guards beat me I take it that he himself is beating me.
(6)   I.e. when I am so disturbed in his presence, what possibility is there of repose in his absence?
(7)   It is written in the Quran that the prophet Jacob became blind with crying at the separation from his son Joseph.
(8)   Because the king always fulfils the hopes and expectations of his people.
(9)   That is to say: In love I have reached the point where I realise all is you — I am not present as an entity but it is you and only you.
(10)  My existence has vanished before your existence.
(11)  In the Orient, large eyes are considered beautiful and described as intoxicating.


## A STORY CONCERNING THE TOTAL ANNIHILATION AND ABSORPTION OF THE SELF IN THE CONTEMPLATION OF GOD BY A LOVER.

I have heard that, affected by a musician's song
A fairy-faced one started dancing:

Due to the fiery-hearted[1] people around him
The hem of his robe was set alight by a candle
And he became distressed and furious.
One of the friends asked what it mattered:
"My friend, the fire burned only your skirt —
It burned me, altogether, from myself."
Throw off egotism if you are a lover
For it is infidelity to remain with friend and with self[2].

## GLOSSARY

(1)  'Fiery-hearted' has been used for the Persian *Sherida*.
(2)  That is to say — in the presence of the beloved the feeling of egotism is infidelity from the state of love.

## A DISCOURSE CONCERNING THE OCCUPATION OF THE PEOPLE OF LOVE

I recall a tale told by a wise and ancient one —
A frenzied[1] person ran away to the jungle[2].
His father, afflicted by the loss, neither ate nor slept;
People reproached his son who replied,
"Since my friend has called me his own —
I do not own to acquaintance with anyone else.
Since the Most High God showed me His beauty
Aside from that, whatever I have seen appears to be delusion!"
He has not strayed who turns his face away from creatures
But has discovered his missing Oneness.
There are some fervent ones beneath the skies[3]
Who can be termed both wild beasts and angels[4].
Angel-like, they do not become heedless of the memory of God

148

But like wild beasts, they flee human beings by day and by night;
They are strong-armed[5] and short-handed[6]
Sagacious, maddened with love, intelligent and intoxicated
Sometimes sewing their patched garments quietly in a secluded corner
Sometimes burning them in ecstasy in an assembly[7].
They have no thoughts about themselves, nor care for anyone
Neither is there a place for anyone else in their corner of belief in Oneness.
They have distracted wisdom and are disturbed in mind;
They stuff their ears with the Adviser's counsel.
The duck[8] cannot drown in a river
What torment would the salamander[9] suffer from punishment by fire[10].
Empty-handed, courageous people
Passing through a wilderness without a caravan —
They do not expect approbation from people
Because they are like that — being the chosen of God Most High is sufficient:
They are hidden from the eyes of all creation and are God's favourites[11].
They are not wearers of the sacred thread and — robed with the mendicants'
habit of patches and shreds
Like a vine they have fruit and shadow[12] in abundance.
They are not wicked and do not dye blue like us[13]
Their heads are on their shoulders like oysters
Not like the river which froths with foam;
They are not only human — bones and skin,
But rather, in every aspect — aware of the intrinsic qualities of God.

Neither is the king the buyer of every slave
Nor is each and every person alive the wearer of patched garments[14];
If every drop of water became a pearl[15]
Markets would have been full of them, like shells;
They do not tie legs to their feet, like jugglers[16]
Because the wooden leg slips fast from its place.
They are the followers of the privacy of the Serai of ALAST[17].
From first draught till the blast[18] of the trumpet they are intoxicated;
Through fear of the sword they will not renounce their aim

149

Because regimen[19] and love are hostile, each to each, like glass and stone

## GLOSSARY

(1) Inspired with the love of God.
(2) Forest or wilderness.
(3) Saints. They appear to be distracted and disturbed.
(4) Because of their worship of God the saints are described as angels. Metaphorically, they are termed wild beasts on account of their apathy and tendency to shun human beings.
(5) Since they possess supernatural powers.
(6) 'Short-handed' is the literal translation. In Persian, it means 'humble'. They have these virtues in accordance with their merit and status.
(7) In a congregation of *Sama'a* (audition).
(8) Duck; standing for people plunging into the sea of unitarianism, who cannot drown.
(9) Salamander, a legendary lizard living in fire.
(10) They are not seekers of paradise nor have they a dread of hell.
(11) They may not be agreeable to mankind in general but they are saints and apostles.
(12) Shadow means protection here.
(13) They are not sinful, putting on the blue dress — the garb of mendicants.
(14) Very many who wear patched garments (dervish garb) are not driven by the spirit.
(15) The saints and apostles are few in number.
(16) Jugglers may tie wooden stilts to their legs.
(17) According to the Traditions of the Prophet, God Almighty assembled all the spirits on the Day of Genesis and enquired from them: "*ALAST BE RUBBEKUM*" meaning, "Art thou not My Creature" upon which all of them replied: "*BALA*" meaning, "Verily it is Thou". Serai means an inn.
(18) According to Muslim belief a *Sur* (Trumpet) will be blown on the Day of Resurrection upon which all of past and present creation will be present alive (Quran Surah LXXIV.7)
(19) As there is hostility between glass and stone, similarly there is hostility between love and rules or vanity and self-seeking.

## A DISCOURSE CONCERNING THE INFLUENCE OF
## ECSTASY AND THE DOMINATION OF LOVE

One had a sweetheart in Samarqand[1]
You would say that she was very sweet of speech
Such was her beauty that it excelled the sun
And the foundations of piety were plundered by her decorum —
God be exalted, so extremely beautiful —
You would be convinced that it was a token of Divine blessing.
When she walked eyes followed her
Hearts of friends[2] devoting their lives to her very breath.
This admirer used to look towards her surreptitiously;
Once she looked at him angrily and said,
'O bare-faced one! For how long will you follow me?
Do you not know that I am not a bird to be entrapped by you?
If I see you again then, with a sword,
I will behead you like an enemy, without hesitation!"
Someone told him (the lover) to change his inclinations.
"Try to look for a more mild beloved —
I do not believe that you will achieve your aim:
It should not be that, through your deep feelings you give away your life!"
Truly mad with love[3] and hearing this reproach
He sighed from the heart with grief:
"Let be, so that the wound of the sword of destruction
Makes my corpse writhe in blood and dust!
Perhaps people will affirm, before enemies and friends alike,
'He was killed by her hands and her sword!'
I do not feel it right to run away (even) from the dust of her street;
Tell her to calumniate me cruelly.
O self-conceited one! You ask me to renounce her —
It is better that you refrain from saying this!
Excuse me: whatever she does
She would do right even if she determined to kill me;
Her heat[4] burns me every night

151

And every morning, her fragrance enlivens me.
If I die in the lane of the friend today
I shall have a tent pitched by her side for the Last Day."

Do not run away from the battle
Because Saadi has immortalised whom love had martyred.

## GLOSSARY

(1)   A famous town in Central Asia.
(2)   Friends means those in love, lovers.
(3)   Frenzied.
(4)   Literally : it is fire.

## A DISCOURSE CONCERNING SACRIFICE OF THE PEOPLE OF LOVE AND TAKING DEATH AS A BOON

A man was breathing his last and he was thirsty[1]:
"Fortunate is he who dies in the water[2]."
An immature person said to him, "How surprising!
When you are dead, what difference is there between moist and parched lips?"
He replied, "Even at the end I do not saturate my mouth
So that I lose any of my sweet life while thinking of it[3].
A really thirsty person plunges into a deep tank
Because he knows that the drowned die fully saturated.
If you are a lover, catch hold of His hem —
If He says, "Give up your life!" then reply, "Take it!"
You will eat the fruits of paradise
When you resolve to pass through the hell of non-existence.
The hearts of farmers remain troubled until
The barn is full; then they sleep peacefully.

n this congregation, that person has achieved his goal
Who in the last moment achieved the goblet of faith.


## GLOSSARY

1)   He was dying of thirst for the Knowledge of God.
2)   He was mumbling like this.
3)   He said that he wanted to moisten his lips with the Knowledge of God so
      that he died gladly thinking of it.


## A DISCOURSE CONCERNING THE RESOLUTENESS AND PATIENCE OF DEVOTEES OF THE PATH

have heard this from the devotees of the Path[1]
That the beggars of God[2] are wealthy.
An old man came out to beg one morning
He saw the door of a mosque and called for alms.
He was told, "This is not the house of a person
Who may give you anything. Don't stay here to make mischief."
The old man enquired, "Whose house is this then
That it does not better anyone's condition?"
He was told, "Be quiet, what erroneous talk is this?
The owner of the house is our God."
He observed the arch[3] and the chandelier
And brought out a heart-rending cry —
"To go from this place would be regrettable;
Frustration at this door is distressing
For I did not return despondent from any lane —
Why should I go ashamed[4] from God's door?
There also will I extend my hand for charity
For I know that I will not return empty-handed!"

I hear that he sat there as an attendant[5] for a year
Keeping his hands raised like a plaintiff's.
One night the foot of his life sank in the bog[6]
Out of weakness, his heart started fluttering[7].
In the morning someone put a light near his head
And saw him at his last gasp like a morning lamp[8].
He was mumbling joyfully and saying,
"Whosoever has knocked at the door of the Benevolent, it has opened
    for him."
The seeker should be patient and forbearing
Because I have never heard of a dejected alchemist
However much money he puts into black soil[9] —
Possibly he may turn copper into gold some day.
Gold is good for the purchase of possessions (but)
You will not be able to purchase anything better than blandishments for
    the Friend.
If you are distressed at the hands of a sweetheart
And someone else is available to console you
Do not lead a hard life due to ill-temper
Extinguish its fire with another water:
But if she has no peer in beauty
For this small torment, do not abandon her.
The heart can be made to retreat for that person
For whom you can curb your inclination.

## GLOSSARY

(1)   *Salik* (Persian) = devotee of the path.
(2)   Because of their freedom from care they are described as 'beggars of God'.
      They appear to be contented but they are always begging God. Since they
      do not have any money or worldly goods they are indigent but because of
      their contentment they are described as kings.
(3)   The arch is the principal place in the mosque and is called the Mihrab. It is
      where the prayer-leader prays and leads the prayers.

) Frustrated.
) *Mujawir* (Persian) = an attendant at any shrine.
) He was at his last gasp — dying.
) Palpitating.
) Since lamps used to burn the whole night long, they had very little fuel left in the morning so they flickered.
) The working substance of alchemists is black.

## A DISCOURSE STATING THAT THE TRUE LOVER DOES NOT SHRINK FROM ENDURING HARDSHIPS

virtuous person prayed the whole night long
nd in the morning he raised his hands to invoke blessings.
voice from heaven told the old man,
You will not gain your wish, go and take your way —
our prayers are not acceptable at this door.
ither leave without grace, or go on imploring humbly!"
he next night he would not sleep for praising God and in Divine worship.
disciple who knew his condition, said
When you know that the door is closed from the other side
o not make futile efforts."
uby-like tears on the face[1]
e shed with intense sorrow and said, "O son!
o not think that if He has pulled at the reins
will withdraw my hands from the saddle-straps!
would have returned frustrated from the way
I had seen an alternate way;
hen the mendicant is refused from one door
nd he knows another way, there is no need to be depressed.
have heard that there is no way for me in that lane
ut there is no alternative on the other side either!"

155

He was in that condition, with head hung to the ground
When suddenly the ear of his heart heard,
"Although he is not skilled yet he is acceptable —
Because for him there is no shelter other than with Us[2]."

## GLOSSARY

(1)   He shed tears of blood.
(2)   Us means God.

## DISCOURSE

Do you know what the man in Nishapur[1] said
When his son slept without saying the Isha[2] prayer?
"O son, if you are a human being, do not expect
That without effort you will ever reach any destination!
The weeds which appear after the barley harvest do not endure
Theirs is a useless crop and of no consequence.
Guard expectations of profit and beware of loss
Because people not anxious about loss are unfortunate."

## GLOSSARY

(1)   Nishapur is in Khorassan, Iran.
(2)   Of the Muslim prayers, Isha is the last of the five 'compulsory' prayers. It
can be described as the prayer of the first watch of the night.

## THE EXERCISE OF SELF-RESTRAINT TOWARDS THE CRUELTY OF A PERSON WITHOUT WHOM ONE CANNOT EXIST

The bride of a youth complained
To a sage old man about her husband:
"Surely you do not approve that with this young man
My life should pass so bitterly!
Other women who are in a similar situation —
  do not find them disturbed like me!
Wife and husband are friends together such
That they are as two kernels and a single shell.
  have not experienced this from my husband in all this time —
Not even once did he smile after first seeing me!"
The auspicious old man heard this talk —
The man of years has understanding —
Sagely he gave her the reply:
"If he is handsome, endure his burden
t is regrettable to turn your face away from such a person
Like whom another is not to be found.
Why do you become refractory, if he is a rebel?
He will write off the name of your existence[1].
You must become resigned to the will of God like any creature
Because you will not see another master like him.

### GLOSSARY

1)   That is to say that you will ruin your life.

### DISCOURSE

One day my heart burned over a slave
Who said while his master was selling him,
"You will get very many slaves like me —
  will not get another one like you."

157

## A STORY CONCERNING A FRIEND'S PREFERENCE FOR AFFLICTION OVER CURE

There was a fairy-faced physician in Merv[1]
Whose graceful height was like a cypress tree in the garden of the heart[2].
He did not know about the hearts he wounded[3]
Neither did he know about his sick eyes[4].
A foreign patient explains,
"For some time I was in love with the physician —
I did not want to be healthy and fit
Because then the physician would not come to see me."
There are very many acute intellects
Which are blunted by the madness of love —
When love wrings the ears of intellect
Discretion does not raise its head.

### GLOSSARY

(1)   Merv is in Central Asia
(2)   He was tall and graceful.
(3)   The wounded hearts of the lovers.
(4)   In the Orient, beautiful eyes are described as sick eyes in poetry and prose.

## THE OVERPOWERING OF INTELLECT BY LOVE

A man made an iron instrument[1] carefully
Because he wanted to try his strength against a lion.
When the lion rent him with its claws
He found he had no strength in his grasp.
A man said to him, "Why are you sleeping like a woman?
Hit him with the iron instrument!"

158

heard the miserable fellow, fallen, saying,
"This is no affray between the lion and the instrument!"
When love overpowers the intellect of the wise —
That is the story of the iron instrument and the lion;
When you are in the clutches of an overwhelming lion
Of what use is the iron instrument to you?
When you fall in love, do not talk of intelligence
Because the ball is a prisoner in the hands of the bat.

## GLOSSARY

1) An iron instrument resembling a hand with which wrestlers exercise by locking
their fingers into those of the instrument.

## THE DIGNITY OF THE BELOVED IN THE EYES
## OF THE LOVER

Two cousins married —
Both charming, beautiful and of noble birth:
She was deeply in love
While he was hateful and refractory[1].
She had a nature polite and courteous as a fairy
He used to keep his face toward the wall
She used to decorate herself
He prayed for death from God[2].
The village elders made the boy sit down:
"If you don't love her, give her back her dowry."
He laughed and said, "An exchange for one hundred goats[3]
That is no loss for being freed."
The fairy-faced one tried to scratch her skin with nails[4],
"I shall never be able to endure leaving my dear one —

159

He relinquishes love, faithfulness and our union.
I have no concern whether he accepts or disavows me;
I shall lead my life in his memory in this manner
That I shall endure the oppression and go on practising kindness.
Not just one hundred goats but even three hundred thousand
I do not need if I cannot see the friend's face."
Whatever it is keeps you from your friend
If you ask honestly, that in fact is your beloved.
A man wrote to a seeker of God,
"Do you pray for paradise or for hell?"
"Don't ask me that question!
I like whatever He likes for me[5]".

## GLOSSARY

(1)   The boy hated the girl.
(2)   The boy was tired of his life.
(3)   The dowry was one hundred goats.
(4)   On mention of the repayment of her dowry, the girl scratched her face and started crying. She would not agree to a separation.
(5)   God.

## A STORY RELATING MAJNUN'S TRUE LOVE FOR LAILA

Someone asked Majnun "O Welcome One!
What happened that you do not come to Hay[1]?
Presumably the love of Laila no longer persists in your mind —
Your ideas have changed and you are no longer in love."
When the poor fellow heard this he started crying bitterly:
"Sir! Leave me alone[2];
Go! My heart is in a pitiable condition
Do not pour salt on my wounds

To remain at a distance is not a test of patience
Because at times distance is necessary."
The other said: "O faithful one of happy disposition!
Tell me if you have any message for Laila."
He replied: "Do not take my name before the friend
Because where she is the very mention of my name is wrong.[3]

## GLOSSARY

(1) Hay is the name of the tribe of Laila.
(2) Literally: Keep your hands off my hem.
(3) A stage comes when the lover annihilates himself into the loved one. To
mention his name before the beloved is a proof of duality.


## THE STORY OF SULTAN MAHMUD, HIS TRUE LOVE
## AND THE QUALITIES OF AYAZ

Someone criticised the King of Ghazna:[1]
"Alas, it is amazing that Ayaz has no comeliness;
A flower having no colour and fragrance —
The nightingale's love for it is strange."
This story was reported to King Mahmud
Who reflected on it and felt distressed:
"O Sir! I love his manners and his ways
Not the beauty of his stature and figure."

I heard that a camel in a narrow passage
Fell down, breaking open a box of pearls
And the king declared it fair game, gave permission for its plunder.
The cavalcade started from there in haste,
The troopers went after the pearls and coral —

161

Intent on pillage they became separated from the king.
None from amongst the ranking and dignified servants
Remained behind with the king, except Ayaz.
He said, "O entangler of hearts in ringlets!
What did you bring from the plunder?" Ayaz replied, "Nothing:
I was following you.
Attending on you, I did not run after wealth."
If yours is an honoured place[2]
Due to honours bestowed, then do not be neglectful of the king.
It is not customary for the saints
To ask God for anything other than God[3].
If your eyes are set on the beneficence of the Friend[4]
While your mouth is open with greed[5] —
Knowledge of the mysteries will not come to the ear of the heart.
The Truth is like a decorated congregation —
Desire and covetousness are dust-raising whirlwinds.
Did you not observe that wherever dust is blowing
The eyes cannot see even if one is clear-sighted[6].

## GLOSSARY

(1)  Sultan Mahmud: whose slave Ayaz was a wise man.
(2)  Literally: you have nearness in a place of audience
(3)  It is not permissible for the saints to ask God for anything other than Him.
(4)  God.
(5)  You suffer from egotism.
(6)  The dust raised by vanity and covetousness conceals the essence of God.

## THE FIDELITY OF PIOUS PERSONS

By chance I and an old man from Faryab[1]
Reached the western territory by the seashore.

had one dirham² — they allowed me to board
But did not allow the dervish to embark.
The sailors set sail and made the boat run like smoke
Because the master of the ship was not God-fearing —
   wept in sympathy for my companion.
Seeing my distress he laughed out loud and said,
'O intelligent one! Do not be anxious about me:
That very Nature⁽³⁾ which is carrying the boat will also bring me!"
He laid his prayer rug on the surface of the water —
I thought it was imagination or a dream —
In my astonishment, I did not sleep that night.
In the morning he saw me and said,
'O blessed friend! You were surprised (but)
The boat brought you, and God brought me."
Superficial observers will not believe
That saints⁴ walk over water and fire;
Is it not so that an infant not understanding fire
The kind mother takes care of him?
People who are engrossed in spiritual ecstasy
Understand in the same way that they are cherished of God.
He preserved Ibrahim from the heat of fire⁵
Like the box saved Moses from sinking in the Nile⁶.
When the child is in the hands of a swimmer⁷
He is not afraid even if the Tigris is wide and in flood.
How can you step onto the surface of a river
Like the saints, when you are a sinner on earth?

## GLOSSARY

(1)    Faryab is an Iranian town.
(2)    A coin.
(3)    God.
(4)    Saints not known to the public are believed occasionally to travel thus in the
       interest of divine administration.

(5)   Ibrahim Khalil Allah or Abraham the Friend of God. He was thrown into
      a fire by Nimrod, the Pharaoh, but the fire miraculously became a bed of roses
(6)   The guardians of the infant Moses put him inside a box and left it floating
      on the Nile to avoid the execution of the infant at the hands of the Pharaoh
(7)   Is in the guardianship of the swimmer.


# A DISCOURSE CONCERNING THE DISAPPEARANCE OF THE CREATED IN COMPARISON WITH GOD'S GRANDEUR

The path of wisdom is nothing but complicated convolution.
To the pious[1] there is nothing other than God —
This may be said to those who know reality
But presumptuous people[2] will find fault with it:
What then is the sky and the earth
What are humans, the herbivorous and the carnivorous creatures?
O sensible person! Your question is a good one
And I will give you the reply, if you appreciate it:
The forests, the rivers, the mountains and the skies
The fairies, the humans, the giants and the angels
Whatever they are, they are still so very much more humble than He —
Not worthy to be described as existent before His substance.
For you the sea is great because of its waves[3]
On account of their height the revolving skies are very high;
But how can superficial observers recognise
That the contemplatives are in a like case[4]?
That if the sun is there, there is not an atom
If there are seven rivers then a single drop is not.
When the King of Grandeur[5] raises the flag
The universe drops its head into the collar of non-existence.

## GLOSSARY

1) Devout persons possessing knowledge of God and His kingdom.
2) One may not understand, but the devout possessing knowledge of God and His kingdom know that the stuff of reality is God.
3) Since superficial observers are denied observation of the Truth, they consider the universe great, but to those who observe Nature and His attributes this universe is nothing.
4) Contemplative people are the saints.
5) If God displayed the attributes of His glory and splendour, all creation would disappear.

## THE STORY OF A VILLAGER'S VISIT TO THE IMPERIAL ARMY CAMP

A village headman along with his son, passed on his way
Near the main camp of the imperial army.
The son saw the heralds, the swords and the battleaxes
Tunics of satin and golden belts,
Hunters and wrestlers with bows and arrows
Quiver-bearing archer-slaves;
Someone wearing fine painted silk,
Someone with a royal cap on.
The son who saw all this grandeur, pomp and show
Found his father very inferior[1].
The father's demeanour deteriorated: he became pale —
Took fright and ran towards a corner.
The son said, "You are, after all, the village chief!
In your own province, you are greater than the lords.
What happened, that you became despondent?
You have started trembling, like a cane in awe of the king."
He said, "Yes, I am the chief and the master —
With all my dignity while I am in the village."

165

Venerable people are terror-stricken[2]
When they go to the court of the king.
O ignorant person! You are still in a village
If you think in terms of rank or honour for yourself

The poets said naught
That Saadi did not relate a parable to it.

## GLOSSARY

(1) Comparatively inferior.
(2) Before venerable and pious people, lesser beings are inferior and without any reality or substance. For the people who have observation of the Most High God in their vista of possibilities, others are absolutely nothing.

## THE STORY OF THE GLOW-WORM

You may have seen in gardens and meadows
A worm glowing like a lamp in the night:
Someone said, "O night-illumining insect!
Why is it that you do not come out during the day?"
And the glow-worm, product of clay
What a wise reply he gave:
"I am out in the forest both by day and by night
But I do not appear in the presence of the sun.[1]

## GLOSSARY

(1) In the presence of the greater reality, every small thing is null and void. Similarly in the presence of the Creator this universe is absolutely nothing.

## THE STORY OF AN INTELLIGENT PERSON AND ATABAK SAAD BIN ZANGI (MAY ALLAH FORGIVE HIS SINS)

Someone eulogized Saad Zangi
(May many Divine Blessings descend upon his grave!)
He rewarded him with riches and garments and patronised him
Giving him a robe of honour in accordance with his reputation
When he[1] saw *Allah-o-Bas*[2] woven in gold
He became frenzied and tore the dress from his body.
He was so madly incensed
That he jumped up and made off into the desert.
One of his companions there asked him
"What did you see, that your attitude changed?
In the beginning, you kissed the earth thrice[3];
Kicking it in the end was not proper."
He laughed and replied, "In the beginning, in fear and expectation,
I started trembling like a reed.
At the end, in awe of the dignity of 'Allah-o-Bas'
Nothing and no human being was within my perception."

### GLOSSARY

(1)  The person who eulogized the king.
(2)  *Allah-o-Bas* = Allah is All. The garments given him by Saad Bin Zangi, the king, had "Allah-o-Bas" woven on them in gold.
(3)  When you arrived at court you kissed the earth three times, in respect for the king, his riches and his wealth — then you abandoned everything and ran away.

## THE STORY OF A PIOUS PERSON

There was a tumult in one of the towns of Sham[1] —
The people arrested an old man of holy disposition:

167

Till now the sound echoes in my ears.
While fetters were being put on his hands and feet
He said, "Till the King does not signal
Who has the courage to plunder?
Such an enemy should be considered a friend
Who I know has been appointed by the Friend for me;
Whether there is honour or dignity or disgrace and imprisonment in store
I consider it to be from Allah and not from Omar and Zaid²."

O intelligent one! Do not be afraid of sickness —
If the physician sends you bitter medicine
Eat whatever comes from the hand of the friend —
Because the sick person is not more clever than the physician.

## GLOSSARY

(1) Syria.
(2) Omar and Zaid is the equivalent of Tom, Dick and Harry.

## THE STORY OF A PIOUS ASCETIC

Someone's heart, like mine, was in the hands of another —
It was pledged¹ and he used to bear very many indignities²
Beyond all intelligence and understanding.
Tambourines were played, declaring him insane³;
He used to tolerate slaps from his friends
Always keeping his forehead projecting like the head of a nail.
His fancy lay over his mind so much⁴
That it cudgelled his brain⁵.
For the sake of the friend, he tolerated injustice from enemies
Because the friend's poison is a sovereign remedy⁶.

He was unaware of his friends' reproaches
As one immersed is unaware of the rain.
He whose heart's foot puts a step on a stone[7]
He does not care about the glass of honour.
One night a incubus made himself fairy-faced
shared the bed with the pious one and consorted with him[8]:
In the morning he could not go to prayers
And amongst his friends, none was acquainted with the secret.
In the morning he went down to the water
But its gate was closed like marble[9] by the cold weather.
An admonisher started to reproach him:
"You will kill yourself in the cold water."
The upright young man cried aloud,
"Look, no mischievous talk, be quiet!
This boy has charmed my heart for some time
And in love for him such a thing happened that I could not restrain myself.
He did not even once out of politeness ask me about my welfare —
See what a burden my heart endures.
Then, He who created my body from clay
Out of His nature put a pious soul in it.
You are amazed if I carry the weight of His orders[10]
When I am always under His beneficence and gratitude."


# GLOSSARY

1)  A pledged or pawned heart is a term used in the East to signify that a person
    is in love.
2)  God involves the pious in various difficulties to test them and for their
    correction. The troubles faced by the pious are in expiation for sins.
3)  Everyone used to call him intelligent and wise, but after this love they
    proclaimed him mad.
4)  Imaginings of the beloved displaced all his ambitions and he was resigned to
    his fate. He was prepared to tolerate every humiliation.
5)  Literally : kicked the heights of his brain.

(6)  Antidote.

(7)  One who strikes his heart against the stone of love no longer cares about dignity.

(8)  That is to say, he had a nocturnal emission (a wet dream), after which it is necessary to have a complete bath to purify the body before going to prayers.

(9)  The water was icebound or closed with snow, so much so that it appeared like a marble door.

(10) Obey His orders.


## A DISCOURSE IN CONNECTION WITH THE AUDITION OF MUSIC BY THE PIOUS AND AN EXPOSITION CONCERNING ITS JUSTIFICATION AND FUTILITY

If you are a lover[1] lose yourself
Or else seek the path of safety.
Be not afraid that love will ruin you
Because you will remain immortal even though it destroys you.
Vegetation does not germinate from clean seeds[2]
First ashes fall on them.
That[3] will introduce you to the Truth[4]
Which will afford you deliverance from your actions;
While you possess egotism, you will not find the inward way
And nobody knows the mystical meaning of this except people in ecstasy[5].
Not only the voice of a singer, but even the sound of hooves beating
Is a song and music if you have love and fervour;
No fly buzzed before anyone with the disposition of a lover
That he might not have beaten his head with two hands like a fly[6];
One with the disposition of a lover does not know the low and the high
    notes[7]
But the dervish[8] starts to cry at the chirping of a bird.
The musician never falls silent[9]
But ears are not always open to hear.
When lovers[10] begin the love of wine[11]

170

They start swaying to and fro at the sound of a water-wheel
Start dancing like a wheel[12]
Start weeping bitterly over themselves like the Persian wheel,
Wishing to entrust themselves to God, to go in contemplation:
When they lose control, they tear their garments to pieces.
O Brother, I will tell you what is music!
But I want to know about the listener, who he is;
If his soul is from the true sign of the zodiac —
The angel is humble[13] before his recreation[14].
If the hearer is a person of play and sport and amusement
Then amusement and pastime will determine his mind.
A good voice makes the true sleeper awake but not an insensible one.
The fragrant morning breeze dishevels a flower
Not the dry wood fit for burning, which the axe will split.
The world is full of music, fervour and noise[15]
But what can the blind see in the mirror[16]?
Do not criticize the confused and drunken dervish[17]
Because he is immersed[18] and so he uses any means of escape.
Have you not seen the camel when the Arab sings?
How cheerfulness brings him to a state of dancing —
When ecstasy is even to be found in the head of a camel
If it is not in a human being, he is an ass.


## GLOSSARY

(1)   A lover of God and a pious person.
(2)   Seeds must go into earth before they can sprout.
(3)   The love of God.
(4)   God.
(5)   Lovers of God.
(6)   When humming, flies beat their wings together. The person having the disposition of a lover of God might beat his head with his two hands.
(7)   Treble and bass.
(8)   Real lover of God.

(9)   Invisible and mysterious sounds/voices continue to descend from the heavens but our ears are seldom capable of hearing them.

(10)  The lovers of God.

(11)  The wine of the knowledge of God.

(12)  In a condition of ecstasy/rapture.

(13)  Powerless.

(14)  Even his non-actions

(15)  Intercourse between God and man.

(16)  Even an atom in the universe can effect music but its audition depends on the virtue/capacity of the listener, so how can one devoid of the light of the revelation of God know?

(17)  Drunken with the love of God.

(18)  When a man is drowning, he throws his hands and feet out in order to be able to catch hold of anything — similarly ecstasy brings the dervish to a state of dancing.


## A STORY

A sweet-lipped young man used to practise playing the reed-flute
Which burned hearts like fire.
Many a time his father shouted at him in a rage
And burnt the flute in the fire.
One night he heard a rendering on the flute by his son.
Hearing it made him confounded and astonished,
Perspiring in the face he said —
"This time this reed-flute has set me on fire!"
Do you not know why people, ecstatic with the love of God and in a
    disturbed condition
Wave their arms in dancing?
The door of events opens up in the heart
And he casts off the world with the shaking of his hands[1];
Dancing is lawful to the person in the memory of his friend[2].
In every fold of his garment there is a truth
Admitted, even if you are an expert swimmer

You can do your best only when you are naked[3]:
Throw away the garments of name, honour and hypocrisy[4] —
Helpless is he who is drowning fully clad
Connection with the world is a veil and your existence is without any result
When you cut off the connections, you will be as free as if dead.

## GLOSSARY

1) When the secrets of the truth of the world of Divine presence start revealing themselves before his eyes, he abandons this world — by shaking his hands.
2) Whosoever becomes aware of the secrets of truth, for him dancing is legal.
3) As long as you do not cast off your superficiality, you will not be able to swim in the ocean of truth.
4) Literally, blue-coloured clothes.

## A STORY

Someone said to the moth "O mean[1] one!
Go, find some more suitable[2] friend for yourself;
Tread such a path that you may have some hope!
You and your love for the candle! Where are you and where is she[3]?
You are not a salamander: do not go around the fire
Because valour is required before a war is fought.
The mole avoids the sun
Because it is ignorance to try one's strength against an iron hand[4].
The one that you know is your enemy
It is not wisdom to make friends with her[5].
No-one would say that you do the right thing
If you sacrifice your life for her sake.
The beggar who asked for the hand of the princess[6]
Received a slap — he nourished a frivolous idea.
How is she going to reckon as friend one like you

When faced with the company of monarchs and kings[7]?
Do not think that such a gathering
Will receive with politeness, an insolvent one like you!
Even if she is hospitable to the whole world
You are indigent and she will be angry[8] with you."
See what that ardent lover, the moth
Said, "If I burn, I wonder why there should be anxiety!
There is a fire in my heart like Khalil-Allah's[9] —
This fire is as a bed of flowers for me.
The heart does not pull at the skirt of the beloved
But her love pulls at the collar of my life.
I do not fling myself into the fire
But the chain of love is around my neck.
I was at a distance from her when she set me ablaze
Not at the moment that she set me on fire.
The friend[10] puts forth all this provocation
Which cannot be told her, out of devotion[11].
Who can criticize me for my friendship with the beloved
When I am ready to sacrifice my life at her feet?
Do you know why my ambition is to give away my life?
If she is there, once I am not: — it is justifiable[12].
I burn for the reason that the best lover is he
Into whom the passion of the friend has entered.
For how long will you tell me that I must make a suitable match;
That I should find some sympathetic companion?
Advising a distressed person is
As if you were to tell someone stung by a scorpion not to weep.
Oh! wonder at — do not advise such a person
On whom you know it will have no effect.
A poor one who has lost control of the reins
Do not tell him to go slow, O son!
What a telling point of mystical significance was made by Sindbad[13]:
'O son, love is a fire and advice is air[14].'
Strong winds inflame the fire

The cheetah becomes malicious through punishment.
When I consider it thoughtfully, I realise that you are harming me
In turning my face towards selfishness."

Shrink from vanity to find a better path; and think it good fortune
Because with egotism you are wasting your life.
Self-conceited people follow those of their own kind,
People who are 'beside themselves' walk on dangerous paths.
When I started this work, from the very outset
I gave away the idea of my head.
One getting beheaded for love is true
Because the avaricious is a lover of self.
Death will waylay me all of a sudden —
So it is better that the beloved kills me;
When death is inevitable for the head
To die at the hands of the loved one were better;
Would you not die miserably one day
It were better that you give up life[15] at the feet of the beloved.


# GLOSSARY

(1)   Mean = detestable.
(2)   Suitable = meet for you.
(3)   Where are you and where is she: there is a great difference between your standing and that of the candle.
(4)   Iron hand: An iron hand is used by wrestlers for exercises by locking their fingers to it and trying to twist it around.
(5)   You know that the candle is your enemy and it will burn you.
(6)   Obviously if a beggar asks for the hand of a princess, he is likely to be beaten.
(7)   The candle is is used to providing light in royal palaces. How is it going to consider a poor lover?
(8)   Literally = hot.
(9)   *Khalil-Allah* or Friend of God was the title of the prophet Ibrahim (Abraham) whom Nimrod, the Egyptian Pharaoh, ordered to be thrown into a fire. The fire became a bed of flowers.

(10) Friend: the sweetheart.
(11) Devotion: sanctity or chastity.
(12) Justifiable: I will be the sacrifice and she remains — that is sufficient for me.
(13) Sindbad: *Sindbad* is a famous book by Hakim Arzani, describing the artifices of women.
(14) Strong winds.
(15) Since one has to die one day, why then should life not be given up at the feet of the beloved.

## A CONVERSATION BETWEEN THE CANDLE AND THE MOTH

I remember that when I was wakeful one night
I heard the moth saying to the candle,
"I am the lover; my burning is relevant —
But why are you weeping and burning now?"
She said, "O my poor lover!
My sweet friend, the honey[1] was separated from me!
Ever since then, sweetness has parted from me
Like Farhad[2] the fire caught hold of me by the head."
As she was saying this, every moment the flood of affliction
Flowed downward over her yellow[3] cheeks:
"O slave of passions, love is not your business!
Neither do you exercise self-restraint nor can you wait.
O imperfect one! You flee from a flicker —
I stand here so that I burn up entirely.
The fire burnt your wing —
Look at *me* that it burned me from head to foot."
A small hour of night had scarcely passed
When a fairy-faced one put the candle out suddenly —
She spoke thus with smoke coming from her head:
"O son, the end of love is like this!
If you want to learn love
You will find relief in death, instead of burning.

176

Do not weep at the grave of the slain friend
Rejoice over the fact that he has been chosen.
If you are a lover, bathe after your recovery from illness[4]
And, like Saadi, wash your hands of worldly desires[5].
A lover never gives up his aim
Even though arrows and stones are hurled at him.
I tell you not, by any means, to put to sea
And if you go, consign yourself to the storm.

## GLOSSARY

(1)  Candles used to be made from beeswax.
(2)  Farhad was the celebrated lover of Shireen. *Shireen* means sweet in Persian.
(3)  The melted wax rolling down is described as tears of the candle and is usually of a yellow colour.
(4)  In the East it is customary to have a bath after an illness which is called *Ghusl-e-Sihat* or the bath of health.
(5)  Leave your selfishness, like Saadi.

# CHAPTER FOUR

# *IN CONNECTION WITH HUMILITY*

## IN CONNECTION WITH HUMILITY

Almighty God created you from dust
So, O creation! Be humble like the dust!
Do not be greedy, a firebrand and a refractory one;
He created you from dust — do not be like fire!
Whenever the dreadful fire has shown its arrogance
The dust has submissively let fall its body
One showed haughtiness and the other humility
From this Satan was created and from that human beings.

## A STORY IN THIS CONNECTION

A drop of rain dripping from the clouds
Felt ashamed when it saw the vastness of the sea:
"Where there is a sea, what am I!
If it is there, then I am nowhere."
When it saw itself with humility
An oyster adopted it and nourished it with heart:
Fate carried on its work to such an extent
That it became a celebrated pearl[1], befitting a king.
It attained sublimeness when it humbled itself;
Knocking at the door of non-existence, it became existent.

## GLOSSARY

(1)   In Persian poetry, pearls are likened to raindrops nurtured by oysters.

## AN ACCOUNT OF A PIOUS PERSON'S HUMILITY

An intelligent young man of chaste habits
Landed at the harbour of Rum.
They saw in him exaltation, the vocation of a dervish and correct behaviour;
His belongings were put in an honourable place[1].
One day the leader of the virtuous told him[2]
To dust and sweep out the mosque
As soon as the traveller heard this
He went out and nobody saw him there again;
The other colleagues[3] and the leader thought
That the dervish had no inclination towards service.
A servant[4] of the mosque met him on the way:
"With your depraved judgement you did a graceless thing,
O self-conceited youth! You do not understand
That people attain a rank of honour through service."
With passion and probity he cried out,
"O heart-enkindling and life-nourishing friend!
I did not see any dust or need to sweep in that mosque:
It was 'I' who was full of dust in that holy place!
I withdrew deliberately
Because the mosque is better without dust and straw."
There is no way for the dervish other than
That he keep his body trodden under foot.
If you seek exaltation, practice humility
Because there is no other ladder to this upper storey.

### GLOSSARY

(1)  A mosque.
(2)  Leader of the virtuous: the Imam or the priest who leads prayers.
(3)  Colleagues: other attendants of the mosque.
(4)  Servant: attendant.

181

# A STORY CONCERNING THE MODESTY OF SULTAN[1] BAYAZID BISTAMI

It is said that once on a festival morning
Bayazid came from his bath —
Inadvertently a large basin containing ashes
Was thrown over his head from a neighbouring house:
He was speaking and his turban and beard were disarranged.
He rubbed the hands of thanksgiving over his face:
"O soul! I am fit for hell —
Why should I express displeasure over a little ash?"
Venerable people never take notice of the self —
Do not expect godliness from presumptuous people.
Greatness is not in reputation and discourse
Magnanimity is not in pretension and arrogance.
On the Day of Judgement you will find that person in paradise
Who demanded spirituality and forsook entitlements.
Humility will elevate the head of your magnanimity,
Arrogance will destroy you.
The ill-tempered arrogant one trips over his head —
If you seek magnanimity, do not look for exaltation.

## GLOSSARY

(1)  *Sultan* means king. Bayazid Bistami was a great saint. In the East, saints are sometimes called kings.

# A SAYING IN CONNECTION WITH ARROGANCE AND ITS AFTERMATH AND MODESTY AND ITS BLESSINGS

Do not look for the path of faith among the arrogant and worldly
Do not look for godliness from self-seeking people;
If you seek honour then unlike mean people
Do not look down upon others.
When can a sensible person think that
There is dignity in arrogance?
Do not look for a more celebrated role than
That people should call you a person of pleasing habits.
If someone like you behaved haughtily towards you,
With the eye of intellect you would not see him great.
Even if you were similarly arrogant —
You would look like the haughty one in your own eyes.
If your standing is high
And if you are sensible, you will not laugh at the fallen:
Sometimes it has happened that the lofty one has fallen
And the fallen have taken his place.
I agree that you are free from faults —
But do not be refractory over my defective self.
One of us is holding the cloth of the Ka'aba[1] in his hands
The other lies intoxicated in the tavern:
If He calls the one[2] who can prevent him from coming?
If He turns the other[3] out who can bring him back?
The worshipper is not powerful on account of his deeds
For the drunkard the door of penitence is not closed.

## GLOSSARY

(1)  The Ka'aba, the building at the centre of the Great Mosque of Mecca, is covered with a cloth.
(2)  The intoxicated person.
(3)  The one holding the cloth of the Ka'aba in his hands.

183

## NARRATION CONCERNING THE PROPHET ISA[1] (MAY THE BLESSINGS OF GOD BE ON HIM) AND AN UNCHASTE DEVOTEE

It is said among story-tellers:
That in the times of Isa[1] (May the blessings of God be on him)
There was one who had wasted his life:
Of ignorance and depravity he was a chief.
Presumptuous, hard-hearted, with blackened character
Due to his uncleanliness even Satan was ashamed of him.
He had spent a useless life —
Since the moment he was born, no-one had received comfort from him.
His head was devoid of sense but was full of ostentation:
His belly was fat from eating morsels of iniquity.
His skirt was soiled because of his deceitfulness.
Through unusual depravity, he shamed his own family;
Neither was he honest like caring people
Nor were his ears like the ears of people listening to good advice.
People used to avoid him like a bad year[2]
And would point him out from afar like the first night of the new moon[3].
Lust and sensuality had burned his stock of unthrashed corn —
He had not saved even a single grain of good repute.
This reprobate had enjoyed the pleasures of life so much
That there was no place left in his character roll for writing.
He was a sinner, self-seeking and lascivious
Day and night, careless, intoxicated and devoid of sense.
It is related that Isa[1] came from the desert:
He passed through the private room of a worshipper of God
And the hermit descended the staircase —
He fell at his feet with his head touching the ground.
From a distance the sinner
Was like a moth, astonished by his[4] splendour.
He reflected with regret and with contrition
Like a beggar in the hands of a wealthy person,

184

shamed, apologizing — quietly in impassioned style —
or the nights carelessly turned into day.
ike a cloud, tears of grief rolling from the eyes:
Ah! Alas! I have spent a lifetime in negligence
squandered the ready money of dear life:
Nothing of virtue came from my hands.
No-one like me should live
because for him, death is better than life!
The one who dies in childhood escapes
or he does not have to feel ashamed in his old age.
Creator of the world! Forgive my sins!
they remain with me, they are bad companions,"
In his corner the old sinner was crying:
O Protector, I need succour!"
And he hung his head from shame,
tears of regret rolling down his white beard.
Elsewhere the devotee, his head full of vanity,
cast his gaze over the sinner:
Why is the wretched fellow following us?
Of adverse fortune, stupid; is he akin to us?
He has fallen with his head in the fire —
His desires and inclinations have destroyed life.
What virtue have we seen from his sinning soul
that he should be with me and Christ?
he had taken his troubles away from here,
because of his deeds he would have still gone to hell.
I feel sick at the sight of his abominable face
and I am afraid his evil influence may involve me.
When all congregate on Doomsday,
O God! Do not judge me with him on the resurrection."
While he was thus engaged a Divine Revelation from the One of
      High Attributes
descended upon Isa[1] (May the blessings of God be on him):
Whether he is learned or illiterate —

185

In My court prayers are accepted.
One spoiled life is crying with entreaty and passion —
Who comes to me with humility
I do not turn him away from the lintel of forgiveness:
I pardon his bad deeds —
By My grace I will take him to paradise.
And if the devotee has a feeling of shame
That he will have to keep him company in paradise
Tell him not to feel embarrassed —
Because he[5] will be taken to paradise and he[6] to hell."
Because the sinner's heart was rent in passion
If he[6] felt haughty over his worship
He does not know the court of the Independent[7].
Submissiveness and humility are much better than arrogance and egotism.
He whose clothes are clean but his habits foul —
He does not require a key for the door to hell[8].
At this lintel, humility and humbleness
Are better than prayer and self-conceit.
If you count yourself amongst the pious, you are wrong[9];
Egotism does not reconcile with godliness.
If you are brave, do not show off your valour —
Because every good rider does not necessarily score a goal.
That unskillful all-in-all is like an onion[10]
Which is so deluded as to think that it is brainy like a pistachio nut[11].
This type of devotion is of no use —
Go and apologise for falling short of worship.
That stupid one did not eat the fruit of worship
If he was good to God and bad with God's creation.
The speech of the wise is worth remembering —
Keep this from Saadi in mind:
A God-fearing sinner
Is better than a devotee displaying his worship.

## GLOSSARY

)  Isa = Jesus.
.)  Bad year: year of famine and drought.
)  People usually point at a new moon.
)  Jesus Christ's.
)  The sinner.
•)  The devotee.
)  God.
•)  That is to say the gates of hell will be open for him and he will not have to wait.
•)  Wrong: literally, bad.
0)  The onion has a 'cover over a cover' and is not a solid thing.
1)  A pistachio nut is quite full and solid. Metaphorically, the poet says that a head like a pistachio nut is more brainy.

## THE TALE OF A SAGACIOUS DERVISH AND AN ARROGANT JUDGE

1 old rags a poor theologian[1]
at in the front row at the court of a judge.
he judge looked at him with displeasure;
he janitor[2] caught hold of his sleeve and said, "Get up!
ou know that your position is not a high one:
it in the lower benches, or go away or stand.
)o not be impudent by sitting in an elder's place —
Vhen you do not have the strength, do not show bravery!
Iot everyone is worthy of presidency,
Ionour is by merit and valuation according to dignity;
Iow you do not require further admonition!
his reproach is sufficient for you
1 spite of appearances, one who has to sit at a lower place
)oes not collapse in misery."
he dervish drew a sigh[3]
And moved to a lower place from where he was sitting.

187

The theologians started altercations[4] —
They started saying "Why ..." and "We do not accept ..."
They opened the door of disorder —
Started raising their necks saying "Yes" and "No":
You would say that cunning cocks in a fight
Contended with each other with beak and claws
One was in a frenzy like a madman, rapt,
Another beat with both hands on the ground.
They became involved in a convoluted problem[5]
From which there was no way out.
The man in old rags in the last row
Growled like a lion in the bushes,
"Firm and real arguments must be marshalled —
Not swelling veins in the neck in disputation!
I also have a bat and ball of words[6]"
They said, "If you know the solution, speak!"
The statement that he made, with the pen of eloquence
Impressed the hearts like an engraving on a jewel.
He took the superficial observations, brought them to reality
And dismissed the claim.
People from every side praised him:
"On your intellect and mind a thousand praises!"
He dealt with the subject at such length[7]
That the judge was bogged down like a donkey in the mire.
He came out of his chamber and taking his own turban
With veneration and kindness sent it to him:
"Alas, I did not discover your dignity —
I did not express thanks in honour of your presence!
I am grieved that with such a wealth of erudition
I find you in this lowly place."
The court janitor came forward in a courteous manner
To put the judge's turban on his head.
But by hand and words the dervish stopped him and asked him to go away:
"Do not put the binding of pride upon my head:

Otherwise tomorrow — towards wearers of old clothes
I will be angry, on account of this turban five yards long;
When they call me 'Master' and 'Elder President'
Then people will appear small in my eyes.
Would the wholesome water change its taste
Whether it is in a golden bowl or in earthenware[8]?
There should be intellect and brains inside the head of a person —
I do not want an excellent turban like you.
A man does not become great due to the size of his head —
The head of a pumpkin is large and it is brainless;
Do not raise your neck on account of your turban and beard
For the turban is of cotton and the moustaches are like grass[9].
People who are merely human beings —
It is better if they stay quiet as a picture[10].
According to the value of one's skills an opportunity must be found:
Do not show your height and ominousness[11] like Saturn.
Is height good for the straws in the door-mat?
Is the peculiarity and nature of sugarcane in them[12].
With this wisdom and mind I cannot call you a human being
Even if a thousand slaves follow you.
Aptly the small shell lying in the mud said,
When a greedy ignorant person picked it up:
'No-one will pay anything for me —
Do not fold me in a silken cloth, in madness.'
A rich person is no better than anyone else on account of his wealth,
Even if a donkey assumes the clothes of cattle, he remains a donkey."
In this way the eloquent man
With the water of words washed the malice from his heart:
An aggrieved person uses strong words.
When your antagonist is defeated, do not be lethargic
When you have the chance, blow out the brains of the enemy
Because the opportunity will give vent to ill feelings.
The judge became so involved in his own iniquity
That he exclaimed, "No doubt it is a hard day."

In perplexity he gnawed at his hands with his teeth,
His eyes fixed on the other like the Greater Bear and the Lesser Bear[13].
At that the young man changed the subject,
He went out and then no one found any trace of him.
The elders in the assembly were in uproar:
"Tell us where this audacious person lives?"
The court herald followed him and ran in all directions:
"Did anyone see a person with such-and-such an appearance and face?"
One said that such a sweet-spoken person
Was known solely as Saadi in the town.
A million praises on him that he said this —
In what a sweet style he expressed the bitter truth.

## GLOSSARY

(1) Theologian: a person well versed in religious laws. Here the poor theologian is Saadi himself.
(2) Janitor: an officer in the courts of the *Qazis* (judges) who made protocol arrangements and instructed people to sit in accordance with their status when the Qazi held court.
(3) Literally: The dervish brought out smoke as if from fire.
(4) Altercations: Absurd reasoning. Everyone started to boast of his own superiority.
(5) Literally: they fell in convolution.
(6) Bat and ball of words: I am also interested in this subject. Is it permitted that I speak?
(7) Literally: he made the horse of words run so much.
(8) Something good does not require a good container.
(9) Metaphorically the poet says, a turban is simply made of cotton and moustaches do not have a greater value than grass.
(10) It is better if they keep quiet, do not pretend and put forward no unfounded claims.
(11) The planet Saturn is very high but astrologers and common people regard it as unlucky.
(12) In height the straws whereof mats are made are also tall like sugar-cane but they do not have the nature of sugar-cane.
(13) The Greater Bear and the Lesser Bear are two stars always pointing towards the tropic of Capricorn.

## A STORY RELATING TO THE PENITENCE OF THE PRINCE OF GANJAH[1]

There was a prince in Ganjah
Who was unworthy, unclean and cruel.
Intoxicated and singing he came into a mosque
Wine in his head and a glass in his hand.
In rooms[2] at the mosque a pious person was staying
Who had a captivating tongue and affable heart;
Some people were gathered there to listen to his preaching —
If you are not learned at least you should listen[3].
When the insolent fellow started his disgraceful behaviour
Those worthy people present became perplexed.
When the king's action is deplorable[4]
Who dares to enjoin what is just?
The smell of garlic overcomes the fragrance of a flower —
The sound of a guitar is drowned by the beat of a drum[5].
If to forbid what is evil is in your hand[6]
Do not sit helplessly by,
And, if you do not have the strength, say so;
Because by advice, even habits[7] may be reformed[8].
When the hand and the tongue do not have the power
People show their resoluteness with prayers[9].
A man started lamenting before the wise hermit;
Putting his head on the ground, he started weeping:
"Once, against this irreligious intoxicated person
Imprecate[10] — for we are helpless[11];
One impassioned sigh from an enlightened heart[12]
Is stronger than seventy swords and battle-axes."
The experienced person raised his hands
And said, "O Lord of the high and the low!
This young man is happy with his times:
O God, make all his time happy!"
Someone said, "O leader of uprightness!

191

Why do you seek good for this evil person?
To wish well to a treacherous one
Is synonymous with wishing ill for the town and the people!"
The prudent man with sharp intellect replied,
"When you do not know the inward meaning of something, do not become
    agitated!
I have arranged matters in order with great supplication
I have appealed for his forgiveness from the Creator of Justice.
For, when he abandons bad habits
Then he will attain eternal bliss in paradise.
The pleasure of wine is for a few days[13] —
Abstention from it gives everlasting pleasure."
The words which the pious person had spoken —
One from those assembled repeated before the king.
In a transport of ecstasy, water came to his eyes like a cloud
And the flood of repentance flowed over his face;
The fire of his ardour burnt his inner self
And modesty sewed his eyes at the back of his feet.
He sent someone to the person of pious appearance
Knocking at the door of penitence for redress and succour
Asking him kindly "To take the trouble of coming so that I may pay homage
    to you —
To get rid of this ignorance and this vitiated character[14]."
The soldiers stood at the door on either side
The eloquent person came to the palace of the king.
He saw sugar[15], candles and wine
Houses full of riches and miserable human beings:
One demented, another half-intoxicated[16];
Someone reciting a poem[17] with a bottle in his hand.
To one side the voice of a singer was loud
And from the other, the saki's[18] voice inviting all to drink.
The companions were drunk with ruby coloured wine
The guitarist as drowsy as the guitar and had his head under his armpit
None was from amongst the exalted friends:

With the exception of narcissus[19], the eye was open

The guitar and the tambourine were in harmony with each other

Moaning and lamentation were in subdued tones.

Orders were given and all was broken into small pieces —

That luxurious pleasure was changed into a relic.

They smashed the guitar and ripped the rod[20]

The singer gave up the idea of singing[21].

In the tavern they started throwing stones at the large earthen jar

They straightened[22] the pumpkin and beheaded it

The wine was spilled and the guitar fell with its face down —

You would say that it was a slain goose bleeding[23]

A small earthen jar was pregnant[24] with wine nine months old:

In the tumult she[25] produced a daughter[26] early.

They ripped the wine-skin from the stomach up to its navel

And on seeing this, the blood-shot eyes of the glasses had tears in them.

He ordered that the stones in the courtyard of the house

Should be stripped and paved with new stones

Because the unguent of red[27] coloured wine

Does not disappear by washing the face of marble.

It were no surprise if the cesspool became intoxicated

Because that day it drank[28] too much wine.

Thenceforward anyone seen holding a fiddle in his hands

Would receive slaps from the people like a tambourine

And if any profligate[29] carried a guitar on his shoulder

His ears were twisted like a tambourine.

The young man whose head had been full of arrogance and egotism

Sat in a secluded corner for prayer like an ancient.

His father had reproached him several times and had told him

To become of gentle character and courteous manners.

He had tolerated strictures from his father; and fetters and prison

For him were not as useful as the advice given.

Had the mild-speaking person been harsh with him

So as to expel the youthfulness and ignorance from his head,

His misconception and his pride would have prompted him

Not to leave the dervish alive.
The roaring lion does not surrender[30]
Thinking of a sharp sword of claws.
With mildness, the enemy can be made a friend
But when you admonish your friend with mildness, you are his adversary
No one became stern of face like an anvil
Who did not feel the hammer of polite behaviour on his head.
Do not show surliness towards the superior
When you find him strict, try to be mild.
Whomsoever you see, treat him with politeness
Whether he be your dependant or superior.
Will this one turn his neck away due to your arrogance?
No, with sweet words he will become more compliant —
It could be a success[31] due to sweetness of tongue
Because the ill-tempered always experiences bitterness.

Obtain pleasant-speaking words from Saadi
Tell the sour-tempered to die in bitterness.

## GLOSSARY

(1)  Ganjah is the name of a town in Iran, near Tabriz. The famous author Nizami
     Ganjavi was from this town.
(2)  There are private rooms inside mosques called *Hujra* or *Maqsura*. The *Imam*,
     leader of the prayers, and the *Muezzin*, person calling people for prayers, and
     other dignitaries on religious visits, use them as resting places.
(3)  This is Saadi's saying. If one is not learned he should listen to the conversation
     of the learned.
(4)  Literally: when the steps of the king are bad.
(5)  Literally: becomes humble before the sound of a drum.
(6)  To forbid evil is the duty of every believer if he has the strength to do so.
     If he has no strength, he should deprecate it and denounce it; and, if he is not
     able to do even that, he must regard it as bad inwardly. These are the three
     stages of *Nahi an al-munkar*.
(7)  Or manners.

3) Literally: become purified.
9) Pious people deflect evil by virtue of their 'Knowing-heart.'
10) Or curse.
11) Literally: we are without hands and without a tongue.
12) Literally: knowing-heart.
13) Literally: for five days.
14) Depravity.
15) In those days it was customary to eat sweetmeats with wine.
16) Viz. some persons were insensible while the others were semi-conscious or half drunk.
17) Verses.
18) Cup-bearer.
19) Metaphorically the narcissus flower is compared with the centre of the eye by poets in the East.
20) The rod used to be a musical instrument with a silken cord on it.
21) Literally: abandoned the idea of singing.
22) They used to store wine inside dried and hollowed-out pumpkins. The poet says that the pumpkin was made to sit and then beheaded.
23) Poetic metaphor. When red wine was spilled it looked like the blood of some slain animal. Since the pumpkin was beheaded, it looked like a slain goose.
24) There was wine in the small earthen jar also.
25) The small earthen jar was 'pregnant' with wine — *Khum-e-aabistan-e-khumr*. And it is of the feminine gender.
26) In Persian literature and poetry, wine is allegorically described as 'the daughter of grapes'. Since the small jar was also broken and the wine spilled it is described as the 'pregnancy having terminated and the abortion of a daughter.'
27) Literally: ruby-coloured.
28) The spilled wine flowed through the cesspool. Metaphorically the poet says that the cesspool drank too much wine that day.
29) Literally: sinner.
30) Literally: does not throw away the shield. Viz. even a brave man is agitated by a severe reprimand.
31) Literally: the ball can be carried away.

## THE STORY OF THE HONEY PEDLAR

A man of cheerful looks used to sell honey
Hearts were inflamed because of his pleasantness.
The sweet-hearts[1], gloriously bedecked
Were his customers, more numerous than the flies.
Even if he had brought poison,
From his hands they would have eaten it like honey.
A jealous person saw his business
And envied the bustle and activity of his trade.
The next day he made a round of the town
Honey on his head and a frown on his face;
He went peddling and calling to and fro
But no fly sat on his honey[2].
When in the evening he had not got any cash
He sat in a corner dejectedly,
Like sinners making wry faces at God's denunciation
Or like the eyebrows of the prisoners on the day of Eid[3].
A woman told her husband jokingly,
"Even honey from a surly person is bitter."
Forbidding is the taste of food from him
Who has eyebrows knitted like a wrinkled tablecloth.
O Sir, do not render your work more difficult —
The bad-tempered man's fortune declines.[4]

I admit that you have no gold or silver
Do not you have a sweet tongue like Saadi?

### GLOSSARY

(1) Sweethearts = admirers.
(2) There were no customers for his honey.
(3) A Muslim festival at the end of the month of Ramadan.
(4) Literally — the bad-tempered person is one with reverted fortune.

## A STORY IN CONNECTION WITH HUMILITY PRACTISED BY THE VIRTUOUS

There was once a pious man —
A profligate[1] drunkard laid hold of his collar:
From the miscreant[2], the man with conscience clear
Took blows but did not raise his head from contemplation[3].
One said, "After all, you are a man too!
Forbearance towards this rude person is repugnant."
The person of chaste nature heard this,
Responded, "Do not tell me such a thing!
When ignorant drunkards tear the collar of a doughty one,
Who thinks in terms of combat with a person with the lion's paw.
The wise do not expect from an intelligent one
That he will lay his hand on the ignorant drunkard's collar.
A virtuous person passes his life thus
That he suffers hardships and does kindnesses."

### GLOSSARY

1) Persian *Rind*. Literally: profligate or loose-behavioured.
2) Literally: black-hearted.
3) Persian *Sukun*. Literally: composure or serenity.

## A STORY CONCERNING TEMPERANCE BY NOBLE SOULS

A dog bit the leg of a hermit living in the desert
With such a fury that poison was dripping from its teeth —
In the night the poor fellow could not sleep from pain.
In his family there was a very young girl
Who scolded her father and was furious:

197

"After all, did you not have sharp teeth[1]?"
Through his pain, the man in the distressed condition
Laughed and said "O, Light of my Heart[2]!
Although I had the strength
I withheld my mouth and teeth
Even if I had a sword's wound in my head
I would not bite the leg of a dog!
From the unworthy, badness can proceed
But a human being cannot become a dog."

## GLOSSARY

(1)  Why did you not bite the dog?
(2)  In literary Persian *babak-e-dilfroz*. *Babak* is said to very young children.

## THE STORY OF A PIOUS MASTER AND CONTUMACIOUS SLAVE

A venerable person skilled in worldly arts —
Had a slave who was ill-mannered;
This evil-favoured person with unkempt hair
Was bad tempered[1].
His teeth were poisoned like a dragon's teeth
Excelling all the ill visaged ones of the town.
Water was always on his face from running eyes[2]
And it was conspicuous. With armpits stinking like onions,
His brows were knitted as he cooked.
When finished he would sit beside his master[3]
Constantly harmonious when chewing bread.
If someone died he would not even serve water.

Harsh reproof or stick had no effect on him —
Due to him the house was disordered by day and night
Sometimes he would throw thorns and straw in the way
Sometimes he threw the hens into the well;
Of frightful countenance
He would not run any errands.
Someone said, "From this bad-mannered slave
What do you want: manners, skill or elegance?
He and his baseness do not deserve
That you tolerate this hardship and bear this burden.
I will bring an excellent well-disposed slave
For you. Take him to the market for slaves[4]:
If someone offers a penny[5], do not refuse it;
If you ask me the truth, he is dear even for no money[6]."
He of good disposition listened,
Laughed and said, "O friend of auspicious origin!
The temperament and behaviour of this boy are defective, yet
Through him my nature will become good.
Putting up with him
I will become able to tolerate the injury and injustice of others.
I do not feel it kind to sell him
And disclose his faults to someone else.
When I will tolerate his evil with moderation
That is better than to make him over to someone else.
Whatever you like for yourself select it for others too[7];
If you are disquieted, do not involve others
Moderation, in the beginning, will appear like poison to you
But it will become honey when absorbed into your temperament.

## GLOSSARY

1) Literally: had vinegar rubbed on his face.
2) Because he had sore eyes, water was always present on his face and his armpits
   were stinking like onions.

(3)   Literally: sit thigh by thigh.
(4)   I will bring for you an excellent well-disposed slave — you take this one to the slave market and sell him.
(5)   *Basij* in Persian. A very small coin.
(6)   He is good for nothing.
(7)   This refers to a tradition which says: "He is a believer who likes for his brother whatever he likes himself."

# THE STORY OF MA'AROUF KARKHI[1] AND A SICK MAN

No one sought the way of Ma'arouf Karkhi
Who did not first put renown out of his head[2].
Once a guest came to him —
Twixt his sickness and death there was a very little distance;
His head was bereft of hair and his face devoid of brightness
Life was hanging to him like a hair.
He camped there and put up his pillow
Starting at once to cry and lament.
Neither could he sleep for a moment[3] during the night
Nor could anyone else sleep for his lamentations.
Distracted in disposition, with a harsh temperament
He would not die himself but people were dying due to him, his quibbling[4]
His wailing, his weeping and restlessness.
People fled from him
If there were any left of the inhabitants of that place
It was the weak one[5] and Ma'arouf only.
I have heard that he[6] did not sleep for many nights attending on the sick
     man;
Ever vigilant, Ma'arouf did whatever he[7] asked.
One night sleep overcame him —
For how long can one endure without sleep —
After a while when his eyes began to sleep
The traveller started talking absurdly:

"Cursed be this dirty breed
They are only after name and honour and they are cheats and impostors,
They are proud and well-dressed,
They are deceitful and sellers of virtuousness.
What does the pot-bellied one[8], unconscious with slumber know
That some poor fellow has not closed an eye."
He said many forbidden things about Ma'arouf
And why he slept inattentively even for a while.
Due to his politeness the Shaikh[9] connived over this
But the ladies in the womens' apartments[10] overheard —
One said to Ma'arouf stealthily,
"Don't you know what the lamenting dervish said?
After this, go and tell him to take his own way:
'Take your misery away and die in some other place!'
Welfare and compassion are all right in their place —
But goodness towards the bad and worthless people is wrong.
Do not put the head of an ignoble fellow on a pillow —
The head of an oppressor should be placed on a stone!
O man of good disposition, don't do good to bad people!
Only a stupid person plants a tree in saline soil.
I do not say one should not take care of others but
Do not waste your generosity on the mean.
Do not be mild and polite to a stingy fellow
As you do not stroke the back of a dog like a cat.
If you want justice, the grateful dog
In disposition is better than an ungrateful human being;
Do not favour a stingy person with iced water
If you do, write its requital on ice.
I have not seen such an enigmatic person
Do not be kind to this worthless man."
He laughed and replied, "O comfort of heart, my wife!
Do not feel troubled with the absurdities of this person;
If with displeasure he shouted about me,
His displeasure sounds cheerful to my ears."

201

Ear should be given the calamity of a person
Who is unable to sleep due to restlessness
When you find yourself in pleasant circumstances and happy[11].
In gratitude endure the burden of the weak
Even if you are yourself like the very form of an enchantment —
Still you will die and your name will die too, like your body.
If you nourish the tree of clemency
You will, no doubt, eat the fruit of renown:
Have you not seen that there are very many tombs in Karkh
But none other than Ma'arouf's tomb is renowned.
Only those people have attained eminence despite wealth
Who have thrown away the crown of arrogance;
Those who like pomp and show practise self-conceit
They do not know that dignity lies in forbearance.

## GLOSSARY

(1) *Ma'arouf Karkhi* was a celebrated saint. Since he was a resident of Karkh, he is called *Ma'arouf-e-Karkhi* or *Ma'arouf Karkhi*.
(2) The first duty of those who want to tread the way of Ma'arouf Karkhi is that they must shun renown and self-conceit.
(3) Literally: could sleep for a breath during the night.
(4) Literally: argumentative.
(5) The patient.
(6) Ma'arouf Karkhi.
(7) The patient.
(8) Ma'arouf Karkhi.
(9) The saint or Ma'arouf Karkhi.
(10) *Poshidagan-e-Harem*. Literally: hidden ones in the seraglio.
(11) Saadi's dictum.

## A STORY CONCERNING THE STUPIDITY OF UNWORTHY PEOPLE AND FORBEARANCE BY THE SAGACIOUS

A vicious person in need went to a sagacious one:
At that moment there was nothing in his purse.
His[1] girdle and hands were clean and empty
That like dust shed wealth on his face.
The shameless petitioner came out
And reaching the street, started reviling him:
"'Beware of these silent scorpions
Blanket-clad, rending 'cheetahs'[2],
That like a cat sit on their haunches[3]
And if any prey is snared they leap up like dogs.
He has brought the shop of fraud towards the mosque
For lesser prey is ensnared at home.
The valorous rob caravans
But they take the clothes off people's backs.
They have sewn black and white patches;
With hypocrisy they have accumulated gold.
What good cheats they are!
World-wandering barn-beggars, blessing people in the night[4];
At the time of prayer don't see them as old and sluggish
Because in dancing and ecstasy they are youthful and alert:
They are the gluttonous[5] stick of Kalim[6]
But they present themselves as feeble.
Neither do they practise abstinence nor are they intellectuals.
It is sufficient that they eat up the world through religion —
They put the cloak of Bilal[7] on their bodies
And with the income of Habash[8], make suits of clothes for women.
You will not see them practising any tradition of the prophet
Except for *Nan-e-Sahar*[9] and an afternoon nap[10].
Their stomach is as replete with morsels
As the mendicant's bag with seventy different kinds[11]."
I do not want to say anything more than this in this respect

203

Because it is defamatory to explain one's conduct.
The ignorant one said much in this vein:
The malicious eye does not observe the virtues.
He, who has disgraced himself too much,
"What respect would he have for others' honour?"
A disciple narrated these matters to the Shaikh[12] —
If you ask earnestly, he was unwise to do so.
"An evil person talked against me behind my back — and disappeared.
The associate who brought and narrated evil tales is worse than the vilifier.
A man shot an arrow and it fell on the way
It did not grieve my body and did not harm me.
You picked it up and brought it towards me
And you are sticking it into my side!"
The sagacious person of good disposition laughed and said,
"It is easier to say more than this. Let him say on.
Whatever he has said: this is a part of my defects;
Whatever *I* know, that is only one part out of a hundred!
Whatever opinion he has formed about me
I know myself that my defects are there.
He has been in contact with us this year only —
How can he know my seventy years of failings,
My vices, better than I? In the world
None except the Omnipotent knows.
I have not seen a person make a better guess
Who thought that these were my only defects.
If on the Day of Judgement he will depose about my sins
Then I am not afraid of hell because my record is fair.
If some adversary describes my faults
Come, tell him to take away the register of my deeds from before me!
Those people have been the pious of God's way
Who have been the target of the arrow of calamity;
Keep quiet till they rend your skin
Because sagacious people endure the burden of evil persons.
If people make goblets from the earth of human beings
The revilers will break them with stones."

## GLOSSARY

1) The hands and the girdle of the sagacious person.
2) Persian *palang*. Literally : a hunting leopard.
3) Interpreting the meditation posture.
4) Persian *Shab-Kok*. Literally : the beggars who stand on some elevated point at nights and bless people name by name.
5) The stick of Moses devoured all the snakes released by the magicians. The stick is, therefore, described here as a glutton.
6) *Kalim* or *Kalim Allah*, meaning Speaker with God. An attribute of Moses, who spoke to God.
7) *Bilal* was an Abyssinian slave who converted to Islam.
8) *Habash* means Abyssinia.
9) *Nan-e-Sahar* means morning food. It refers to the food taken before dawn by Muslims during the fasting month of Ramadan.
10) It was traditional for the Prophet to sleep awhile after lunch.
11) A mendicant's bag has many patches on it.
12) Shaikh here means the sagacious person.


# A STORY CONCERNING THE IMPUDENCE OF DERVISHES AND FORBEARANCE BY KINGS

King Saleh, one of the kings of Sham[1]
Used to come out in the early morning with a slave;
He would roam about the markets and streets
With half his face covered in the Arab style.
He was discerning and held dear the dervishes —
Whosoever has these two qualities, he is a virtuous king[2].
He found two dervishes sleeping in a mosque,
Found them distressed and disturbed in mind —
Due to the coldness of the night they had been unable to sleep
And were waiting like chameleons[3] for the sun to rise.
One of the two was saying to the other,
"On judgement-day there would need to be some mediator

If these kings with arrogant necks
Who are busy in amusement, luxury, affectation and coaxing
Were to go to paradise with the poor —
Then I would not raise my head from under the bricks of my grave.
The abode of the blessed is our property and place —
Because today we have the fetters of grief on our legs.
What comfort did you get from them all your life
That you should undergo hardships even in the life hereafter?
If near the wall of paradise, Saleh there
Were to come, I would break his head with a shoe."
When the man spoke thus and Saleh heard it
He did not find it expedient to stay there.
Some time passed ere the fountain of the sun[4]
Washed slumber from the eyes of creation.
The King sent someone for both of them
Sat in state and made them sit with honour
Showered the rain of munificence over them
Effaced the traces of privation from their bodies —
After suffering from cold, rain and floods
The two sat with renowned commanders of the army.
The beggars who had passed the night without cover
Were perfuming their clothes over a pot burning aloes-wood:
One of them asked the king gently,
"O one whose commands are obeyed by all the world[5]!
Favourites attain exaltation —
From us, your slaves, what was it that pleased you?"
The king was delighted[6],
Laughed before the dervish and said,
"I am not one who on account of his pride and dignity,
Frowns on helpless people —
You also get rid of your ugly disposition towards me
So as not to be discordant in paradise!
Today I have opened the gates of peace
Tomorrow do not you close the door on me!"

f you are fortunate adopt this way
f you want eminence hold the hand of the dervish.
No one obtained a fruit from the boughs of Tooba[7]
Who did not sow the seed of goodwill today.
f you do not have goodwill, do not look for prosperity
The ball can be carried only with the bat of attendance.
How can you get the splendour of light as from a candle
When, like a Qandil[8] you are charged with the water of self-conceit.
That substance accords light to the congregation
n the heart of which there is a burning like a candle.

## GLOSSARY

1) Syria.
2) There is a play of words here. *Saleh*, in Arabic, means virtuous. The king's
   name was also Saleh.
3) Literally: meditating like the chameleon waiting for the sun to rise. The
   chameleon keeps his eyes open and is stated to be gazing towards the sun.
4) I.e. the sun rose.
5) Literally: with a ring in his ear. In the East it was the custom to put a ring
   in the ears of slaves.
6) Literally: opened up like a flower from a bud.
7) *Tooba* is the name of a tree in paradise bearing delicious fruit.
8) A *Qandil* was a glass pot into which water and coconut oil were poured and
   lighted.

## A STORY CONCERNING THE DEPRIVATION OF THE SELF-COMPLACENT

There was one who had a little knowledge of astronomy
But was arrogant with his head intoxicated with pride.
He came a far distance to Koshiar[1]
His heart full of belief and his head full of vanity.

The wise man closed[2] his eyes on seeing him
And did not teach him a single letter of knowledge.
Remaining empty-handed he decided to return home:
Then the eminent one told him,
"You have imagined yourself to be full of wisdom;
The pot[3] which is already full — how can it be filled again?
Leave your pretensions and become empty to be filled!
You are full of egotism, therefore you are returning empty."

From life[4] in the world — in the manner of Saadi —
Become devoid and then return full of knowledge.

## GLOSSARY

(1)  Shaikh Abul Hassan Koshiar was a celebrated astronomer. He was the guide
     and preceptor of the great Avicenna.
(2)  I.e. would pay him no attention.
(3)  Or self. When one is conceited, the head is full of pride, how could there be
     room for knowledge in it.
(4)  I.e. forget your self and lose your subjectivity first.

## A STORY CONCERNING RESIGNATION AND RIGHTEOUSNESS

A slave in a rage with the king became disorderly and deserted.
The king ordered a search to be made for him, but none found him;
When he returned, on account of anger and strife
The king asked the executioner to spill his blood.
The bloodthirsty, unkind executioner
Drew his dagger like a thirsty tongue.
With wounded heart, the distressed one said:
"O God, I forgive him!

Because I have always remained in his grace and favour
In his blessings I was rich.
It may not be so tomorrow[1] for my blood —
They may catch the king and his enemies will be happy."
When his words came to the king's ears
His anger subsided and the cauldron of his anger ceased to boil
The king kissed the slave's head and his eyes, many times;
He became a standard-bearer with drums and kettle-drums —
Due to mildness in that dreadful place (the battlefield)
Destiny made him reach such a rank of honour.
The purpose of this tale is that mild speaking
Works like water on the heat of a fiery person.
Have you not observed that, in the field of swords and arrows[2]
They put on the hundred-layered kaftan[3]?
O friend! Be polite to the ill-tempered enemy
Because mildness blunts the cutting sword.

## GLOSSARY

1) Tomorrow: the Day of Resurrection.
2) Field of battle.
3) A *kaftan* was a cloak made of hundreds of layers of pure silk cloth. The sword could not cut through the kaftan in battle.

## A STORY ABOUT HUMILITY AND SUBMISSIVENESS BY THE PIOUS

Amid desolation, where a sagacious person in tatters lived
A man heard the howling of a dog.
In his heart he said, "Why is there a dog here?"
And went inside the hut to find the righteous dervish.

He found no trace of a dog in front, or at the rear
And other than the wise one he saw nothing.
He began to leave guiltily
Because he felt guilt at probing the secret.
The holy man heard the sound of footsteps from inside
And said, "Hullo, why are you standing at the door? Come inside!
O light of my eyes! Do you not understand
That the dog which barked from this place is *I*?
When I saw that it was submissive[1]
I turned pride, opinion and wisdom out from my head
Like a dog cried out at His gate too much
For, I did not see a more miserable creature than a dog!"
If you want to achieve an exalted status
From the humility of civility you would reach a great height.
In this court of audience they achieved supremacy
Who kept their status low.
When the torrent came with fury and horror
It fell from the height headlong into the abyss
When dew fell miserable and small
See, the sun carried it to Capella[2].

## GLOSSARY

(1) Literally: when I saw that He bought humility.
(2) Capella is a first magnitude star in the constellation Auriga. That is, the sun took the dew to the highest heaven.

## A STORY CONCERNING HATIM 'THE DEAF'[1] AND HIS HUMILITY

A group of historians[2] are unanimous on this —
They do not believe that Hatim was deaf.
Early one morning there was the buzzing of a fly
Which had become ensnared in a cobweb.

All the spider's weakness and stillness was a fraud —
The fly thought it sugar, but it was a chain.
The Shaikh[3] looked towards it — by way of example:
'O prisoner of greed, stay!
Not everywhere are there to be found sweets, honey and sugar —
In many corners there are snares set and traps!"
One from amongst the assembly of thinkers said:
'O pious one on the way of God! I am astonished
That you heard the noise of the fly?
For it came to our ears with difficulty.
Since you perceived the buzzing of a fly
After this you ought not to be called deaf!"
Smilingly he responded, "O one of acute intellect!
One deaf is better than he who listens to frivolous talk.
Those who are my personal companions
Are the concealers of defects and the diffusers of skill
When they hide my moral defects —
Egotism will subdue me and pride will make me vile.
I pretend that I do not hear
So that by this pretence I may get rid of blemishes.
When companions take me to be deaf
They narrate all my habits, good and bad.
Since listening to my bad points is repugnant to me
I will save my self from bad habits."
Do not fall into the well due to the rope of admiration —
Be deaf, like Hatim, and listen to the bad reports.

He did not seek good fortune and security
Who turned his neck from Saadi's advice —
What better counsellor do you need?
I do not know whose advice may come to you after his.

211

## GLOSSARY

(1) Should not be confused with Hatim the Generous. Hatim 'The Deaf', was Abdel Rahman Hatim, a pious person. It is related that when once a woman was saying something to him that she chanced to break wind and was so ashamed and perplexed that she put her head between her knees. Pretending to be deaf, Abdel Rahman Hatim asked her to speak a bit louder as he was hard of hearing. Ever after he pretended that he was deaf.

(2) Literally: eloquent persons.

(3) Abdel Rahman Hatim.

## THE STORY OF A PIOUS MAN AND A THIEF

There lived on the outskirts of Tabriz[1] a respectable man
Who was always wakeful and would say his midnight prayers.
One night he saw a thief with a rope ladder
Rolled up which he threw into the corner of a terrace of a roof.
He informed his neighbours and there was a hubbub:
People assembled from every side with sticks in hand.
When the thief heard the voices
He did not risk staying in danger —
He was frightened by the din[2]
And thought it opportune to run away quickly.
The tender-hearted pious man took pity
On the poor night thief who was thus deprived.
He overtook him in the dark
And encountered him from the other side
Saying, "O friend, do not run! I am your friend!
I am as the dust of your feet in bravery
I have not seen anyone like you for fortitude.
A battle is fought in two ways only:
One is to face the enemy boldly;
The second is to save one's skin from the battlefield.

In both these two eventualities I am your servant —
What is your name, O Master? I am a slave of your name.
If you so wish after consideration,
I will take you to a place I know.
It is a small house and the door is well-secured
I think the master of its goods and chattels is not there
We will put some bricks[3] one on top of the other —
Then putting one's feet on the other's shoulders
Be satisfied with whatever comes to hand;
It will be better than to return empty-handed."
By such encouragement, flattery and contrivance
He drew the thief towards his own house.
The night-rambling youth gave him the support of his shoulder
And the master of wisdom climbed up.
Cap, turban and whatever property he had
He threw into the thief's skirt from above
And then from there shouted, "Thief!"
"O Youth, it is a matter of assistance and reward."
The cunning thief jumped out because of the noise
And ran with the belongings of the pious man under his arm.
The heart of the virtuous man of faith was satisfied
That the disturbed one had achieved his objective.

The wicked person took no pity on anyone —
The heart of the virtuous took pity on him.
It is not surprising in the disposition of the intelligent
That they behave politely towards the wicked out of goodness.
In the blessings of the pious the wicked persons are mentioned[4]
Although the wicked do not deserve goodness.

## GLOSSARY

(1)  Tabriz is a city in north-west Iran which was founded by Zubeida, wife of the Caliph Haroun El Rashid.

(2)  *Gir-o-Dar* Literally: take him, hold him.

(3)  Literally: clods.

(4)  It is in the Traditions of the Prophet that if the pious and virtuous had not been in the world the wicked would have been destroyed.


## THE TOLERANCE OF VIOLENCE FOR THE SAKE OF A FRIEND

A man had a simple heart like Saadi —
He was in love with an innocent one.
He would tolerate the reproaches of adversaries
Which would rebound like a ball from a hard bat
He would never frown at anyone
And would not grieve at being ridiculed.
A man said to him, "Do you not feel the affront
Do you not feel these slaps and stones?
The mean keep their bodies slippery,
The weak endure their enemies.
A mistake by an ignorant one should not be pardoned
Otherwise people will say that one lacks manliness and courage."
The desperate lover replied well —
A reply such as is worth writing in gold:
"My heart is the place for the love of friend
There is no capacity left for malice towards anyone."

## A STORY

What a nice thing of Bahlul[1] of blessed disposition to say
As he passed by a contentious devotee:
"If this claimant of exaltation had recognised the Friend
He would not have involved himself in the wranglings of adversaries.
If he had found the clue to the existence of God
He would have treated all creation as non-existent!"

## GLOSSARY

(1)    *Bahlul* means one who laughs heartily, a cheery person. But here it refers to
*Bahlul-e-Dana*, a famous saint during the times of the Abbasside Caliphs. He
pretended to be insane.

## THE STORY OF LUQMAN[1] THE WISE AND A
## RESIDENT OF BAGHDAD

I have heard that Luqman the Wise was of dark complexion,
Not self-indulgent and delicate of body.
One man mistook him for his slave
In Baghdad — and put him to work with mud and clay.
For one year he was building a house for the man
And none from amongst the slaves of the master recognised him.
When his own escaped slave returned to him
He was greatly afraid of Luqman.
He fell on his knees and asked to be pardoned.
Luqman laughed and said, "Of what use is apology?
For one year my heart bled due to your violence
How can I suddenly turn it out of my heart?
But, O good fellow, I do pardon you!

215

For your benefit caused us[2] no loss.
You inhabited your women's apartment
My wisdom and knowledge increased.
O one of good fortune! I too have in my possession a slave.
Sometimes I gave him hard work to do —
I will not oppress his heart any more
When I remember the hardships of my own labour with clay.
Anyone who had not experienced the rigours of the aged
Would not burn over weak assistants.
King Bahram spoke thus to his vizier:
"Do not make subordinates work unduly hard
If the words of your superiors sound harsh to you,
Do not be severe on underlings."

## GLOSSARY

(1) Luqman = a wise man. A famous Eastern fabulist (supposed by some to be the same as Aesop).
(2) Us here means 'I.'

## JUNAID[1] OF BAGHDAD AND A STORY OF HIS CHARACTER AND REFINEMENT

In the desert of Sanaa, Junaid
Saw a dog lacking its canine teeth[2]
From a strength of grasp capable of holding lions
It had become powerless, like an old fox[3].
After running down and catching deer and wild goats
It was getting kicked by the goats of the tribe.
When he found it miserable, weak and wounded
He gave it half of his provisions.

216

I have heard tell that he said in a flood of tears:
"Who knows which one of us is better off?
Apparently I am better than he is today —
Let us see what destiny brings upon my head:
If the foot of my belief does not stumble from its place[4]
Then I shall put on my head the crown of God's remission;
And, if the knowledge of God
Does not remain in my body, then I will be humbler than he.
For the dog when dead[5], despite its ugly name
They will not take *it* to hell."

Saadi[6], this is the path of the people of the Way of God
Who did not look into themselves expecting grandeur;
For this reason they excelled the angels
That they did not consider themselves superior to a dog.


## GLOSSARY

(1)  A celebrated saint.
(2)  The dog had become so old that it had lost its canine teeth.
(3)  It is said that the fox does not seek prey herself but eats from the leftovers of other animals' kills.
(4)  I.e. if I were to be proved honest on the Day of Judgement.
(5)  Paradise and Hell are for human beings.
(6)  This is the saying of Saadi.


## THE STORY OF A HOLY MAN AND A HARPIST

An intoxicated person had a harp under his arm
In the night he broke it on the head of a pious man[1].
When it was day that pious gentleman
Took a handful of money to the lout.

217

"Last night you were haughty and devoid of sense —
Both your harp and my head broke.
My hurt is better and I no longer have any distress;
Yours will not be better without money."

For this reason, God's friends are the leaders
Because they bear so much from the God's created.


## GLOSSARY

(1)   He played the harp all night.


## A STORY CONCERNING THE PATIENCE OF GENTLE PEOPLE
## TOWARDS ACTS OF VIOLENCE BY UNWORTHY ONES

It is said that an eminent one in Wakhsh[1]
Had confined himself to a secluded corner.
He was in fact a free man[2] and not just a sagacious person clothed in rags.
He spread his hand before all creation asking for necessities:
Good fortune had opened its doors to him
But others' doors were closed before him.
A stupid, impudent one attempted
With wanton talk to revile the pious man.
"I seek protection from fraud, pretence and swindles
That sit like a demon on the seat of Solomon[3]
Constantly cleaning their faces like cats
Greedily preying on street mice —
Performers of religious worship only for renown and deceit —
The sound of hollow drums travels far."
He spoke thus and people were gathered around him,
Men and women, ridiculing and laughing about it.

218

But the intelligent person from Wakhsh cried,
"O God! Afford him Divine guidance and penitence
And if he has spoken the truth, O Holy God,
Help me so that I avoid ruination.
I like these words from my fault-finder
In that he revealed my bad habits to me."
If you are as your enemy says, do not be grieved —
If you are not, tell him to go on raving.
If some stupid person says a musk stinks
Be satisfied that he has spoken out of confusion;
And if this talk concerns an onion
Then say, "Yes". Do not indulge in unproductive arguments.
It is not the concomitant of wisdom, opinion and sense
For a sensible person to be deceived by a juggler.
The one who accomplishes his task discreetly:
*He* prevents adversaries from speaking against him.
Do you remain of good conduct, so that the malevolent
Have no opportunity of finding fault with you.
When you feel offended by adversaries' tongues
Do not be severe on your subordinates.
I do not consider anyone more agreeable than the one
Who exposes my real blemishes to me.

## GLOSSARY

(1)  *Wakhsh* is a town in the province of Badakhshan in Afghanistan.
(2)  Was in fact free of worldly connections.
(3)  It is said that the ring of Solomon was stolen by a demon with the help of a slave-girl. He governed the country for some time with its help. Here it means that imposters have occupied the seat of the wise by deceit and fraud.

## THE STORY OF THE COMMANDER OF THE FAITHFUL, ALI, AND HIS DISPOSITION TOWARDS CIVILITY

Someone brought a problem before Ali[1]
Thinking that perhaps he might solve his difficulty.
Amir[2], the imprisoner of enemies and the conqueror of lands
Gave him a reply in accordance with wisdom and knowledge.
However a man in that assembly
Said, "O Abdul-Hassan[3], it is not like that!"
The celebrated Haider[4] was not displeased
Saying, "If you know a better answer than this, then speak!"
The man told what he knew and related it properly —
The fountain of the sun cannot be concealed in the mud[5].
The King of the Valiant[6] approved his reply:
"I was mistaken, he is right
He has given a better solution than I and there is One learned
Better than Whose doctrine there is no knowledge."

If any current master of dignity had been there[7]
He would not have cared to listen by reason of his haughtiness;
And his chamberlain would have turned him out of the hall of audience.
He would have been beaten unnecessarily —
"You are not to disgrace anyone after this
It is lacking in etiquette to talk before the elders[8]."
One with vanity in his head —
Never imagine that he will listen to the truth;
He feels displeased with knowledge and distressed by advice.
Tulips[9] do not sprout from the stones after the rains
But have you not observed that from the wretched earth
Flowers burgeon and the dawn of spring blooms.
O learned one! Do not scatter your sleeve full of pearls
Wherever you see the master full of egotism!
Such a one is not acceptable to the people
Who glorifies himself too much.

Do not speak yourself so that thousands may speak of your virtues:
When you have spoken yourself, do not expect anything from anyone else.

## GLOSSARY

(1)   Ali was the son-in-law of the Prophet. He was the fourth Caliph known as the Commander of the Faithful.
(2)   *Amir* is a title of Ali. The word *Amir* is an abbreviation of *Amir-ul-Monineen*, which means the Commander of the Faithful.
(3)   A patronymic appellation of Ali.
(4)   A patronymic appellation of Ali.
(5)   Viz. that a true thing manifests itself.
(6)   Literally: *Shah-e-Mardan* (Persian), the king of valiant ones, heroes. A title of Ali.
(7)   Saadi's saying starts from here.
(8)   They would say this while giving him a beating.
(9)   Tulips obviously sprout not from stones but from the earth.

## A STORY OF THE COMMANDER OF THE FAITHFUL, OMAR IBN EL-KHATTAB[1], MAY THE BLESSINGS OF GOD BE UPON HIM

I have heard that once in a narrow place with a beggar
Omar kicked the back of his foot[2].
The poor dervish did not know who he was
Because an injured person cannot tell the difference between an enemy and
        a friend;
He became enraged and said, "Perhaps you are blind."
The discreet chieftain Omar said,
"I am not blind, but it was a mistake —
I did not know, please forgive me."

How just the venerated of the faith have been
Who were like this towards their subordinates

221

The chosen intelligent ones are humble in temperament
The branch laden with fruit puts its head on the ground[3]
The polite will arrive at their status tomorrow[4]
The heads of the proud will be bent from shame.
If you are afraid of the day of reckoning
Pardon them who are afraid of you.
O powerful ones! Do not be violent with subordinates
For there is a hand even above your own hand.

## GLOSSARY

(1) Omar Ibn El-Khattab was the second caliph of the Rashida Caliphate.
(2) In poetry, if it is not possible to finish a sentence in the first verse, it is carried forward to the second verse. The couplet here means that in a narrow place Omar put his foot over the back of a beggar's foot i.e. kicked him.
(3) Due to the weight of the fruit the branch bows towards the earth.
(4) The Day of Reckoning.

## A STORY

There was a virtuous one of good disposition
Who would call even the ill-mannered good.
When he died someone saw him in a dream —
Asked to narrate his adventures
He opened his mouth, laughing like a flower,
Started melodiously as a nightingale:
"They did not treat me with harshness
Because I was not severe with anyone."

## THE STORY OF DHUL-NOON[1] MISREE OF EGYPT (MAY GOD BLESS HIM) AND HIS HUMILITY

The tale is told that the water-carrier[2], the Nile
Did not offer water to Egypt[3] one year.
A group of people started towards the mountainous country
Supplicating humbly, seeking rain;
They wept so much that a river started flowing from their tears[4] —
Mayhap the skies might weep over them[5] also.
One from amongst them took the information to Dhul-Noon
That the people were in great hardship and distress:
"Be kind and pray for the helpless
Because the prayers of the chosen are not rejected!"
It was said that Dhul-Noon had escaped to Madain[6]
Not much time had passed before it rained —
The news reached Madain after twenty days
That the dark-hearted cloud had wept[7] over the people.
The old man immediately resolved to return
Because with the flow of the spring season the lakes had become full.
A devout person asked him privately
"What was the philosophy behind your going away?" He replied,
"I have heard that for birds, ants and beasts of prey
Their daily sustenance is less due to the evildoing of sinners
I reflected deeply and in this country
I did not find a greater wretch of a person than I myself
So, I got out, lest due to my vices —
The gate of welfare did not close on the congregation[8]."

You will be respected by people only when[9]
You do not consider your own particular 'self.'
The noble who regarded himself with humility
He achieved eminence in this world and in the world hereafter
From this[10] family that slave has become chaste
Who became the dust at the feet of some humble one.

223

O one who passes by our ashes!
By the dust of the ancestors, please remember
That if Saadi became dust what sorrow was that for him
Because in life, too, he was dust.
Humbly put his body down under the earth —
Although he roamed the world like a wind
Not much time will pass ere the soil will consume him
And the winds will again carry him to and fro in the world.
Contemplate that ever since the garden of spirituality opened
No nightingale has warbled more melodiously in it;
It would be astonishing, therefore, if such a nightingale dies
And no flowers were to bloom over its bones.

## GLOSSARY

(1) Dhul-Noon or the fisherman was the title of an eminent Saint in Egypt. It happened that during a voyage someone accused him for the theft of a pearl He was innocent and prayed to God, whereupon many fishes appeared or the surface of the water with pearls in their mouths. He took a pearl and gave it to the one who had accused him.
(2) The flooding of the Nile makes Egyptian soil fertile and there is little rain ir Egypt. Here the poet calls the Nile the water-carrier of Egypt.
(3) One year there was no flooding of the Nile.
(4) I.e. they wept so much that a spring or river of tears started to flow.
(5) Maybe it will rain.
(6) Madain, a town in ancient Egypt.
(7) That it had rained after all.
(8) On the people.
(9) This is Saadi's dictum.
(10) The sons and descendants of Adam.

# TEACHINGS OF RUMI: THE MASNAVI

Abridged and translated by E. H. Whinfield.

With an Introduction by Idries Shah.

Jalaluddin Rumi's great work, *The Masnavi*, was 43 years in the writing. During the past seven hundred years, this book, called by the Iranians 'The Koran in Persian', a tribute paid to no other book, has occupied a central place in Sufism.

> '*The Masnavi* is full of profound mysteries, and a most important book in the study of Sufism – mysteries which must, for the most part, be left to the discernment of the reader.'
>
> *F. Hadland Davis*

> 'To the Sufi, if not to anyone else, this book speaks from a different dimension, yet a dimension which is in a way within his deepest self.'
>
> *Idries Shah*

> 'The greatest mystical poet of any age.'
>
> *Professor R. A. Nicolson*

> 'It can well be argued that he is the supreme mystical poet of all mankind.'
>
> *Professor A. J. Arberry*

THE OCTAGON PRESS
LONDON

## MAHMUD SHABISTARI: THE SECRET GARDEN

Translated by Johnson Pasha from the Aga Khan version.

This book, by an almost unknown Persian sage of the thirteenth century, is among the greatest classics of spirituality of the East.

Though written over six hundred years ago, as a reviewer correctly pointed out, 'Shabistari's ideas can usefully be applied to our own contemporary social problems'.

John A. Subhan says of it:

> 'his work is important out of all comparison . . . because it is a compendium of Sufi terminology in the form of question and answer'.

## HAKIM SANAI: THE WALLED GARDEN OF TRUTH

Translated and abridged by David L. Pendlebury.

For over eight hundred years, in the East at any rate, *The Walled Garden of Truth (Hadiqa)* has been constantly read and enjoyed as a classic and a Sufi textbook.

Professor Arberry quotes Sanai on his own *Hadiqa* as saying:
> 'Henceforward, so long as men have speech at all, the philosophers of the world will read this book!'

> '. . . useful on any level one is able to grasp hold of it – and very enjoyable too'.

*Books and Bookmen*

THE OCTAGON PRESS
LONDON

# THE SUFIS

by Idries Shah.

*The Sufis* is the pivotal work which heralded the revelation of the astonishing richness and variety of the Sufi thought system and its contribution to human culture contained in Idries Shah's many books on the subject.

Today, studies in Sufism, notably through Shah's research and publication, are pursued in centres of higher learning throughout the world, in the fields of psychology, sociology, and many other areas of current human concern.

'For the vital and concentrated knowledge contained in his writings, the work of Idries Shah must be considered a major cultural and psychological event of our time.'

*Psychology Today*

'Must be the biggest society of sensible men there has ever been on earth.'

Ted Hughes, *The Listener*

THE OCTAGON PRESS
LONDON

# TEACHINGS OF HAFIZ

Translated by Gertrude Bell; Introduction by Idries Shah.

Hafiz of Shiraz is unquestionably in the front rank of world classical poets. As a lyricist and Sufi master, his work is as celebrated from India to Central Asia and the Near East as are Shakespeare, Dante or Milton: Goethe himself, among many other Westerners, was among the master's admirers.

As Professor Shafaq says:

> 'Hafiz attained perfect mystical consciousness: and his spiritual and mental power derived from this. The Path, projected by Sanai, Attar, Rumi and Sa'di each in his own way, is described by Hafiz with the very deepest feeling and highest expressive achievement'.
>
> *History of Persian Literature*, Tehran

This collection is by the eminent linguist and explorer Gertrude Bell who (as Dr. A. J. Arberry says) "early in her adventurous life conceived an enthusiasm for Hafiz which compelled her to write a volume of very fine translations".

**THE OCTAGON PRESS**
**LONDON**